kitchen stories
anyone can cook

kitchen stories

anyone can cook

Our Favorite Recipes for Every Day

PRESTEL

MUNICH · LONDON · NEW YORK

To home cooks, everywhere.

Table of Contents

Our Story

It all began with a simple idea: Encourage more people to get cooking at home. Although eating is such an integral part of our lives, many people lack the time, inspiration, and kitchen confidence to make their own meals. So, to help others (and ourselves) overcome these obstacles, we founded Kitchen Stories – a cooking platform to inspire any cook, filled with a range of recipes from easy to more challenging, detailed step-by-step instructions, and engaging videos. Our motto? Anyone can cook.

As recent college graduates, we had limited work experience. Potential investors laughed at our idea: There were enough competitors on the market already – what exactly would we do differently? Nevertheless, we had faith. We decided to pursue our idea, selling our cars and borrowing money from friends and family to get it started. Using a rental home as our set, we produced the first 100 recipes in 14 days. Six months later, we released the first version of our app. Today, we have more than 17 million users worldwide.

Although our home is the digital world, we've always loved the idea of making a cookbook. In these pages, you'll find the same sentiment we've had from the beginning: "Anyone can cook." This cookbook is here to inspire you to make weeknight meals that are anything but boring. For many of the dishes, you'll need only 30 minutes, for some only 5 ingredients, and others only a single pot. Alongside our all-time favorite Kitchen Stories recipes, you'll also find new dishes developed exclusively for this very book.

Happy cooking!

Verena & Mengting

About the Book

When we decided to go for it – to publish a cookbook for the first time ever – we grappled with our approach. Firsts are significant, and we wanted our debut to not only be memorable, but true to who we are as a brand and a community. So there were lots of questions about how to translate our tech-driven, digital mindset onto the printed page.

It turned out that it wasn't quite as complicated as we thought. After all, our mission is simple: To empower people to cook. So it was essential to us that our cookbook be as useful as possible – it should be as intuitive and easy to navigate as our apps, and filled with recipes that are both appealing and approachable, no matter the reader's entry point.

We settled on dinner as the theme for the same reasons. After all, it's the meal that's most challenging for home cooks – even we, a team of food editors and chefs, get into ruts of boredom and laziness. So with a special emphasis on dishes you can cook throughout a busy week, every recipe within these pages can be made in less than an hour, including prep and cooking time. There's no clever calculation to make it so, it's just how it's designed.

Flipping through the pages, you'll find ideas that will restore your faith in what a weeknight dinner can be: from staples of the quick-and-easy arsenal, like pasta bakes and stir-fries, to meals you'd be proud to serve at a dinner party and surprised to find out work just as well on a Tuesday night. Trust us, you've got this.

Chapter structure

This cookbook is divided into six chapters, starting with an overview of a few foundational skills and terms we consider essential for the recipes included. You might be learning these for the first time, or perhaps you could simply use a reminder as you're cooking of the difference between mincing and dicing, or the right roasting temperature for root vegetables. Either way, you'll find Chapter 1 is a great foundation from which to dive into our recipes. Here, we'll also cover the basic tools and pantry ingredients we think every kitchen should be outfitted with for utility and variety, plus a few novel ideas from our chefs and editors.

The remaining chapters (2–6) are dedicated to our recipes. You might recognize some of them from the Kitchen Stories app, including recipes from our community, of which we feature one per chapter. We've made room for these time-tested favorites here because, to be honest, our first cookbook would be incomplete without them – they're classics. In addition, you'll find a range of new, cookbook-exclusive recipes mixed in throughout to ensure you'll never be short on ideas or inspiration when it's time to get cooking.

Hero recipes

Each recipe chapter starts with a "hero" dish, so named because it's especially adaptable according to the ingredients you have on hand and your personal taste. We dedicate extra pages to these in order to go in-depth on the dish, its preparation method, and how to swap in other ingredients as desired. The book's hero recipes will turn out to be the workhorses of your kitchen – think of them as formulas from which you can derive countless fantastic meals from one single foundation.

Recipe instructions

For every recipe in this book, including our heroes, you'll find a chef's note that includes helpful information about how to prepare the dish successfully. We recommend you read these and the instructions in their entirety before starting the cooking process. This will ensure you're equipped with all the information you need to succeed and won't be thrown any curve balls along the way.

Recipe directions are matched with step-by-step photos, just like in our app, to guide you through and help you visualize the process. On the same set of instructional pages, you'll also find extra tips now and then, with quick bits of information on topics such as how to adapt, store, and swap in alternative utensils or ingredients for the recipe – or even a QR code from which you can jump to related content in our app, like videos and guides.

Icons

If you're looking for a quick way to decide if a recipe is right for you, the best way is to refer to the icon key, found in the upper left or right corner of each recipe instruction page. The key will indicate basic information about the recipe in a simple, digestible way.

Here you'll find a summary of all the icons featured in the cookbook. Recipes will always include a summary of the total preparation and cooking time first, followed by up to two more icons, for example diet (vegan, vegetarian, or low carb) and seasonality (the season in which a dish is best eaten according to its ingredient list).

"Make ahead" shows that a dish can be prepped in advance to finish later, while "Crowd-pleaser" and "Family-friendly" hint that a recipe scales well for a large group or is suitable for kids and adults alike. Lastly, "From the community" denotes that a recipe was originally submitted to our app by one of our community members, and has now become a tried and true weeknight favorite.

25 minutes	Vegetarian	Vegan	Low carb
From the community	Crowd-pleaser	Make ahead	Family-friendly
Winter	Spring	Summer	Fall

Essential Utensils

General Utensils

1 Cutting board
2 Knives (chef's knife, paring knife, bread knife, knife sharpener)
3 Box grater
4 Fine grater
5 Rubber spatula
6 Whisk
7 Metal spatula
8 Ladle
9 Slotted spoon
10 Tongs
11 Cooking spoon
12 Vegetable peeler
13 Colander
14 Measuring cups
15 Mixing bowls
16 Aluminum foil
17 Parchment paper
18 Kitchen towels

Cooking Vessels

19 Frying pan, 10–12 in. (25–30 cm)
20 Heavy-bottomed, ovenproof pot
21 Pots and saucepans
22 Baking dishes
23 Baking sheets

Appliances

24 Kitchen scale
25 Immersion blender
26 Food processor
27 Food thermometer

Our Pantry Staples

In the fridge
- [ ] Butter
- [ ] Milk
- [ ] Eggs
- [ ] Parmesan cheese
- [ ] Yogurt
  (or sour cream)
- [ ] Miso paste
- [ ] Condiments (mayo,
  mustard, hot sauce)
- [ ] Ginger
- [ ] Lemons (or limes)
- [ ] Something pickled
  (capers, olives,
  pickles, prepared
  horseradish)
- [ ] Fresh herbs (parsley,
  mint, dill, cilantro,
  basil)

Staple vegetables and alliums
- [ ] Potatoes
- [ ] Garlic
- [ ] Onions
  (red and yellow)

In the cupboard
- [ ] Sugar
- [ ] Flour
- [ ] Cornstarch
- [ ] Honey

Sauces
- [ ] Soy sauce
- [ ] Worcestershire
  sauce
- [ ] Fish sauce

Canned goods
- [ ] Crushed or whole
  tomatoes
- [ ] Coconut milk
- [ ] Beans or chickpeas
- [ ] Tomato paste

Oil and vinegar
- [ ] Olive oils
  (one for serving,
  one for cooking)
- [ ] Vegetable oil
- [ ] One sweet vinegar
  (apple cider or
  balsamic)
- [ ] One sharp vinegar
  (rice, red, or white
  wine)

Dried goods
- [ ] Beans
- [ ] Lentils
- [ ] Bouillon powder
- [ ] Pasta
- [ ] Noodles
- [ ] Rice
- [ ] Nuts
- [ ] Seeds

15 Essential Spices to Always Have on Hand

ALLSPICE Warm allspice adds a special something-something to a variety of dishes from stews and meaty braises to desserts.

BAY LEAVES Mild and herbal, bay leaves are great for long-simmering soups and stews. Always pull them out before serving, as the leaves themselves aren't edible.

BLACK PEPPER Sharp and pungent, black pepper is a ubiquitous seasoning often paired with salt to finish off just about any dish.

CARAWAY This slightly aniseed-like spice can be used whole or ground in sweet or savory baked goods, braises, and casseroles.

CHILI FLAKES Made of dried and crushed red chili peppers. Sprinkle chili flakes on dishes as a spicy garnish or let them linger in stews and sauces.

CINNAMON Sold ground or as whole sticks, cinnamon is often relegated to sweet baking projects but makes a delicious addition to savory dishes, too.

CORIANDER Citrusy and subtly sweet, use whole or ground in curries or on roasted vegetables and meats.

CUMIN Whether used whole or ground, this is a warm and nutty spice that works well in curries, soups, marinades, and sauces.

CURRY POWDER A spice mix typically composed of coriander, cumin, turmeric, and fenugreek, curry powder that can add a kick of flavor to roasted vegetables, simple fried eggs, and many other dishes.

DRIED OREGANO Unlike many other herbs, oregano retains its sweet and earthy flavor when dried. Add a pinch to salad dressings, pizza, or pasta sauce.

DRIED THYME Like oregano, thyme retains its slightly lemony, minty flavor when dried. If replacing fresh thyme with dried, use less, as dried thyme is even more pungent.

FENNEL SEEDS With a licorice-like flavor and subtle sweetness, fennel seeds are delicious when paired with roasted meats and vegetables, as their flavor really emerges when heated.

NUTMEG Too much nutmeg can overwhelm a dish, so err on the scant side. Rather than going for ground, try buying whole nutmeg and grating it fresh when adding to dishes.

PAPRIKA Ranging in flavor from sweet to hot, paprika can be used to add a subtle or strong spiciness and smoke to soups and stews.

SALT A fundamental seasoning found in every kitchen around the world. We recommend using kosher or fine sea salt for everyday cooking, and a fancier, flaky salt for garnishing.

Pantry Items We Couldn't Live Without

"In my kitchen, I find a dash of flavored olive oil can never hurt. My favorites are lemon- and garlic-infused olive oils for pesto, gremolata, chimichurri, and other herby sauces."

KRISTIN

"Bonito flakes are an important part of Japanese cuisine – one of my favorites to cook at home. As a natural flavor enhancer, they're great for seasoning dishes and for making dashi, a stock that's the basis of many Japanese dishes."

CHRISTIAN

"In my kitchen, you'll always find Thai chilis and chili flakes, which I toss through pasta sauces, over roasted vegetables, and into pots of beans. I like to freeze fresh Thai chilis to make them easier to keep on hand."

DEVAN

"Nutritional yeast is always stocked in my kitchen. It's not an active yeast, but a seasoning that gives food more flavor and depth. I use it in sauces and soups, and even sprinkle it over pasta dishes."

JULIA

"I'm addicted to tinned anchovies packed in olive oil. I layer them onto sliced tomatoes and sourdough, drop them into pestos or Caesar dressings, blend them with olive oil to make an umami-punched pasta sauce, or eat them solo, late at night."

RUBY

"Fried onions can provide texture to almost any dish – plus, a little sprinkle can even save dishes that may not have turned out perfectly."

LISA

"My security in cooking comes from a jar of chili crisp. I eat it with almost everything, from cucumber salad and boiled eggs to pasta, rice, and dumplings."

XUECI

"Since a vacation in Styria (southern Austria) where they make really high-quality pumpkin-seed oil, I can't do without it. This creamy, dark green, and nutty oil enhances any salad and is amazing with a scoop of vanilla ice cream."

JOHANNA

"I almost always have preserved lemons in the pantry, which lend an intense citrus flavor and mild tartness to pasta sauces, roasts, stews, salads, and dressings. A little goes a long way, so I start by mincing a quarter lemon and adding more as needed."

JULIE

The Foundations

Master the Foundations of Everyday Cooking

In this chapter we've pulled together the knowledge of our chefs and editors to give you concrete and helpful step-by-step instructions for everything from holding a kitchen knife properly to how (and why) to blanch vegetables. Read through the tips and tricks found within the coming pages anytime you feel you need to build or balance out your foundational home-cooking techniques.

Basic knife skills every home cook should know

Many a weeknight meal begins at the cutting board. Our essential set of knives is short and sweet: a chef's knife, a smaller vegetable or paring knife, a serrated bread or utility knife, and a knife sharpener. Each knife has its own benefits and you'll want to choose a different one depending on what you're slicing and dicing.

A chef's knife is perhaps the most versatile and important knife in your arsenal and makes a quick job of everything from chiffonading herbs to chopping an onion or slicing a steak, whereas a smaller vegetable or paring knife is more suited to tasks like hulling strawberries, peeling tough fruit or vegetable skins, or scoring meat. A serrated knife is more versatile than you might think, and should by no means be relegated only to slicing bread. Use it for slicing tomatoes, sandwiches, melons, or heads of lettuce.

How to roast

Consider a pan-fried chicken breast, blanched broccoli, or boiled potatoes. While all taste perfectly good just as they are, they take on new, crisped-up dimensions when finished with a roast in the oven. Countless other ingredients benefit similarly from being roasted until cooked through and golden-brown. The ideal time and temperature depend as much on the ingredient as the consistency and taste you want to achieve. Our introduction and suggested recipes are a great starting point to help hone your skills.

How to pan-fry and sauté

So many recipes begin with pan-frying or sautéing. Put simply, both techniques deal with cooking ingredients in a small amount of fat – typically oil or butter. Pan-frying usually means dealing with larger portions – say, a whole chicken breast or long spears of asparagus –

for snow peas, carrots, green beans, broccoli, and – as you'll see in the pages that follow – many more.

How to cook classic pantry staples

In the many recipes within this book, you'll find us circling back to a few staples served up in different ways – they might feature in soups, as sides, or as key components of a dish. To help you succeed every time, you'll first need to familiarize yourself with some basic knowledge: What does the ratio of rice to water need to be, do you need to rinse drained noodles, and how exactly do you cook dried beans? Our overview shows you eight foundational tips for pasta, polenta, quinoa, rice, rice noodles, dried beans, and lentils, as well as methods for toasting seeds and nuts, so you can feel confident preparing them any which way.

whereas sautéing tends to refer to smaller pieces of ingredients cooked over a higher heat and stirred frequently (think a diced onion, ground beef, or sliced mushrooms). Despite the slight variation in method, both approaches are commonplace and easy to master.

How to blanch

For the novice cook, the prospect of blanching can seem daunting. However, the word simply refers to the process of briefly submerging ingredients (especially fruit and vegetables) into boiling water. This flash-cooking method helps to draw out their flavor and intensify their color, while allowing them to retain their crisp-tender bite. It's also helpful for other applications like peeling tomatoes, making the skins far easier to slip off. Though not suited to all fruits and vegetables, blanching is an excellent technique

The Basic Knife Skills Every Home Cook Should Know

1 How to stabilize a cutting board

Before any ingredient hits your cutting board, you need to make sure it's stable. Some cutting boards already have little plastic feet on them so they won't slip, but for those that don't, here's the easiest way to make sure they are secured: Dampen a paper towel and lay it flat underneath your cutting board.

2 How to hold a knife properly

You will have more control if you hold a knife with your thumb touching the blade and the rest of your fingers pressing against the edge of the handle. It's also important to use your free hand in the correct way. To protect yourself from cutting your fingers, curl the fingers of your free hand into a claw to secure the ingredient you're cutting. Press your knuckles up against the blade and treat them as a guide for the knife.

3 How to slice

To slice a tomato, hold it against the cutting board with your free hand and use a serrated knife to make thick or thin slices. To slice a potato, hold it against the cutting board with your free hand and use a chef's knife to cut a thin slice off it. Turn the potato with your free hand so the sliced edge meets the cutting board and stabilizes the potato as you slice it length- or widthwise, thickly or thinly.

4 How to chop

Whether you refer to the end product as chopped, cubed, or diced, every variation of a "chop" starts with slices. To dice a stalk of celery, for instance, use your knife to halve the stalk lengthwise, then turn the stalks perpendicular to your knife and, using your free hand to hold them, chop the celery into small cubes. A "rough" chop generally means that it's not important for all the pieces to be the same size.

5 How to chiffonade

Chiffonading herbs will give you beautiful long strips of aromatic greenery to thread through dishes or garnish them with. To chiffonade basil, pluck all the leaves and stack them directly on top of each other. Roll them lengthwise, then turn the roll so it's perpendicular to your chef's knife. Slice the roll into thick or thin lengths all the way through. Use your hands to zhuzh them up and separate the pieces before using.

6 How to mince

To mince ingredients like garlic or ginger, start by slicing, then roughly chop into pieces using a chef's knife. Place the palm of your free hand on top of the knife near the tip and rock the knife back and forth over the chopped pieces. Use the edge of the knife to gently scrape the pieces into a pile and rock the knife back and forth over and over again until the pieces are very small. You can also use this technique with fresh herbs.

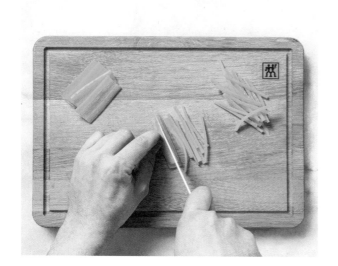

7 How to julienne

To julienne something is simply to cut it into long, thin pieces – like a matchstick. For an onion, this would be as simple as halving and slicing it thinly, but for something like a carrot or cucumber, a julienne is a much more demanding type of cut. To julienne a carrot, peel it and then use your knife to slice it thinly into long rectangles. Stack the rectangles, then slice lengthwise into thin strips.

HERE'S HOW TO SHARPEN YOUR KNIVES AT HOME.

How to Roast

1 The process of roasting should begin with a hot oven, so choose your temperature – for vegetables, aim high at around 400 °F (200 °C); for meats, try a slower, lower roast at around 325 °F (160 °C) – adjust the oven rack as needed, and set the oven to preheat. Prepare your ingredients by chopping them into equal-size pieces so they roast evenly, or simply leave them whole for a longer roast.

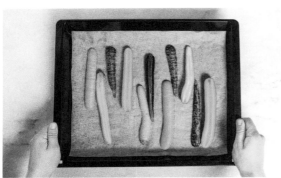

2 Toss or place your prepared ingredients onto a baking sheet with a low rim (ideal for vegetables) or into a baking dish (well suited for large hunks of meat). Make sure that the ingredients have enough room around them, as ingredients that are too tightly packed next to each other, or the rim of a dish, will steam, not roast.

3 Drizzle with oil or another high-heat-tolerant fat and season with salt, pepper, or various spices to your taste. See our list of 15 essential spices on page 17 for inspiration.

4 Transfer your cooking vessel and ingredients to the oven and roast until golden or mahogany-brown on the outside and tender and cooked through on the inside, tossing and rotating as needed for more even browning. If you're not sure how long your ingredients will take, just keep a close eye on them, checking them visually (or with a food thermometer for meats) every 5 minutes after they've been roasting for 15 minutes.

5 Things to Roast

CARROTS

CHICKEN LEGS

CAULIFLOWER

BRUSSELS SPROUTS

BUTTERNUT SQUASH

How to Pan-Fry and Sauté

1 To start, decide whether you will leave your ingredients whole or chop them into equal-size pieces. This will determine whether you will pan-fry (using a lower temperature) or sauté (using a higher temperature and tossing more often). Prepare your ingredients as needed, seasoning meats with salt, pepper, or other spices.

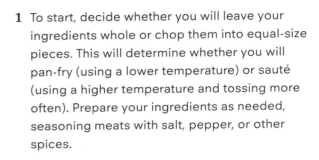

2 Preheat your trusty frying pan over medium heat (to pan-fry) or medium-high (to sauté), then add vegetable oil or clarified butter. Let that heat until the surface shimmers, then grab your ingredients – it's time!

3 Gently add all the ingredients to the pan (laying bigger items such as whole chicken breasts away from you to avoid splattering yourself with any hot fat). If sautéing, immediately distribute the pieces around the pan using a cooking utensil; if pan-frying, don't touch the ingredients at all after adding to the pan. Let everything get nice and brown, adjusting the heat as necessary to keep a strong sizzle.

4 If pan-frying, flip your ingredients once the first side is golden-brown and let them continue to cook until the second side matches the first. If sautéing, keep everything moving often using a cooking spoon, spatula, or a gentle shake of the pan. Season the ingredients with salt and pepper if you didn't already, and remove them from the pan once they're done to your liking.

5 Things to Pan-Fry or Sauté

MUSHROOMS

BROCCOLI

SHRIMP

GREEN ASPARAGUS

RED ONIONS

How to Blanch

1 Set a large pot of water over medium-high heat and bring to a boil. Bubbles should rise quickly from the bottom of the pot and break the surface of the water – that's how you know the water is boiling.

2 While you're waiting for the water to boil, prepare the ingredient you want to blanch – wash it and chop it if needed. Also prepare your station for "shocking" or cooling down your ingredients, whether that's in a large bowl of ice water or in a colander set in a clean sink with access to very cold running water. Shocking the ingredient after boiling stops the cooking process and helps to retain color and crunch.

3 Season the boiling water with salt, then gently add your prepared ingredients using a slotted spoon. Use the spoon to move the ingredients around every so often, but know that, depending on the ingredient, a blanch could be completed after anywhere between 30 seconds (for tomatoes) and 5 minutes (for green beans).

4 The best way to know if your ingredient is finished is to check the texture every 30 seconds. Once they are very vibrant in color and still crisp but tender to the bite (be careful when checking!), use the slotted spoon to transfer everything to your prepared bowl or drain in the colander and run under cold water until cool to the touch. Drain well and pat dry before using or storing.

5 Things to Blanch

SUGAR SNAP PEAS

TOMATOES

ZUCCHINI

SWISS CHARD

GREEN BEANS

How to Cook Classic Pantry Staples

1 Pasta or wheat noodles
Bring water to a boil and salt generously. The ratio of pasta to water should be approx. 1:10. Cook pasta until al dente, according to the package instructions. Drain but don't rinse or toss with oil – we want the starch to stay intact and help bind the noodles with the sauce.

2 Polenta
Bring water, vegetable broth, chicken stock, or milk to a boil in a saucepan. The ratio of polenta to liquid should be approx. 1:4. Slowly pour in polenta and whisk until fully incorporated. Simmer polenta over low heat, whisking constantly for approx. 20 min., or according to the package instructions. Serve with grated Parmesan cheese, butter, salt, and pepper, or as you like.

3 Quinoa
Rinse quinoa under running water until the water is clear. Drain well, add rinsed quinoa and water (the ratio of quinoa to water should be 1:2) to a saucepan, and bring to a boil. Once boiling, reduce heat to low, cover, and let simmer for approx. 15 min., or until the water is fully absorbed. Fluff with a fork and let rest, covered, for approx. 10 min. more.

4 Rice
For most types of rice, use a ratio of 1:2 rice to water. Add rice and water to a saucepan and lightly salt, if desired. Cover and bring to a boil. Then reduce the heat and let simmer for approx. 20–25 min., or until the water is fully absorbed. Fluff with a fork.

5 Rice noodles

Add rice noodles to a heatproof bowl. Bring some water to a boil, then pour over the noodles, stirring to loosen them up. Let sit until tender and cooked through. Drain and rinse under cold water to stop the cooking process, then toss with some roasted sesame, vegetable, or olive oil to prevent them from sticking together.

6 Dried beans

Soak dried beans in plenty of cold water overnight, covered with a kitchen towel. Drain, add to a saucepan, cover with fresh water, and cook according to the package instructions. For a quicker result, add dried beans to a pot, cover with water, and bring to a boil. Cover and let sit for approx. 1 hr, then drain and cook as you would the dried and overnight-soaked beans.

7 Dried lentils

Rinse lentils under running water until the water is clear. Drain well, transfer to a pot, and cover lentils with water. Bring to a simmer over medium heat. Depending on the variety, let cook for approx. 15–40 min., or according to the package instructions. Once cooked, season with salt, and serve with olive oil, vinegar, herbs, or lemon juice.

8 Toasting nuts and seeds

Heat a frying pan over medium heat. Add nuts or seeds and toast until they're aromatic and golden-brown, swirling the pan often to prevent burning. Alternatively, spread the nuts or seeds on a baking sheet and roast at 350 °F (180 °C) for 5–8 min., or until aromatic and golden-brown. Always keep an eye (and nose) on the stove or oven, as nuts and seeds can burn quickly.

Salads & Soups

The perfect weeknight salad bowl

Vegan

Make ahead

"The 'perfect weeknight salad bowl' is so simple because it's actually nothing more than a delicious medley of leftover ingredients. The variations are endless and you can easily substitute one ingredient for another based on what you have. On the following pages, you'll find numerous ideas to help create your own perfect salad bowl.

My recipe includes a selection of my favorite ingredients: Creamy avocado meets crunchy cucumber, while sweet potato brings earthy and sweet notes, and the onions add a pungent kick. Sometimes I add a hard-boiled egg or smoked salmon for an extra serving of protein."

– Johanna

4 servings

FOR THE SALAD
1 lb (500 g) sweet potatoes
1½ oz (40 g) sunflower
  seeds
7 oz (200 g) pearl barley
1 head romaine lettuce
1 cucumber
2 avocados
¾ oz (20 g) mint
olive oil for drizzling
salt
pepper

FOR THE QUICK-PICKLED ONIONS
1 red onion
2 tbsp white wine vinegar
½ tsp salt
1 tsp sugar

FOR THE DRESSING
½ tsp mustard
1 tbsp agave syrup
2 tbsp white wine vinegar
½ cup (120 ml) olive oil
salt
pepper

1 Preheat the oven to 325 °F (160 °C). Peel sweet potatoes and cut them into ⅓ in. (1 cm) pieces. Transfer them to a baking sheet, toss with olive oil, and season with salt. Let roast in the preheated oven for approx. 20 min. Take the baking sheet out of the oven and push sweet potatoes to one side. Add sunflower seeds to the other side of the sheet, then return it to the oven and roast for another 10 min.

2 In the meantime, fill a saucepan with salted water and bring to a boil. Add pearl barley and cook for approx. 30–40 min., then drain and rinse under cold water.

3 Peel and dice red onion. Mix onions with white wine vinegar, salt, and sugar in a small bowl and set aside. Chop romaine lettuce and slice cucumber. Halve avocado, remove pit, thinly slice lengthwise, and roll up into roses. Mix together mustard, agave syrup, and remaining white wine vinegar in a bowl, then slowly stir in olive oil. Season with salt and pepper.

4 Arrange sliced vegetables, roasted sweet potatoes, and pearl barley in serving bowls. Drizzle with the dressing and sprinkle with roasted sunflower seeds and fresh mint.

6 Steps to the Salad Bowl of Your Dreams

For many of us, a healthy and balanced diet is something to aspire to, yet the prospect of salad for dinner is one that's often associated with strict diets and very little pleasure. But the truth is, salad is versatile, quick and easy to prepare, and has the potential to be filling and satisfying – if you know how to do it right.

(Pseudo-) Grains

Let's start with the base for a filling salad: (pseudo-) grains. Pseudo-grains aren't grains botanically, but can be used just like them – think quinoa and buckwheat. Despite their rather mild taste, this foundation for your healthy dinner provides texture and carbs, plus the choices are endless: While most of us will have rice at home, which makes it an easy first pick, spelt provides a slightly nutty taste and is chewier, while millet or couscous are finer in texture. Personally, I also think that pearl barley is totally underrated and makes a great base for hearty salads. Don't know how to prepare these ingredients? Just follow the package instructions, or take a look at our Foundations section on page 41.

Leafy greens

Instead of reaching immediately for butterhead or iceberg lettuce, experiment with alternative options like bitter radicchio or chicory, or leafy vegetables such as Swiss chard, baby spinach, and kale. The choice you make here will help you determine the best dressing for your salad bowl: Delicate leaves such as lamb's lettuce go very well with a lighter vinaigrette, while sturdy romaine hearts can complement creamy dressings, and bitter leaves can be paired with something on the sweeter side.

Vegetables

Vegetables in a salad bowl don't only provide you with vitamins, but bring the seasons to your table. Get inspired by a walk to the market and pick seasonal produce: Go for asparagus in spring, grab some aromatic tomatoes in summer, and when fall rolls around, go for pumpkin or Brussels sprouts. Your selection doesn't need to (and sometimes shouldn't) remain raw, and can also be pan-fried, blanched, baked, or pickled. Another rather unusual but just as tasty option is fruits like berries, figs, or peaches. New cutting techniques can also bring variety of texture and presentation to your salad routine, and now might just be the right time to practice your julienne outlined on page 27.

Proteins

You can choose from a range of animal or plant-based proteins. Chicken, salmon, and shrimp are certainly classics, but you can still vary them by

using different preparation methods. Instead of leaning on the pan-fried chicken breast, try poaching and shredding it. Well-seasoned or marinated tofu or chickpeas will get crispy when prepared in a frying pan or in your oven.

Vinaigrettes and dressings

You've come this far and already picked a balanced selection of ingredients for your salad bowl. Right before the finish line, why buy a dressing from the supermarket, which will often contain a lot of sugar, salt, and flavor enhancers? The base for a homemade vinaigrette is foolproof and really easy.

The classic ratio is 3 parts oil to 1 part vinegar. If you like it more acidic, stick to a 2:1 ratio instead. Experiment with different oils and vinegars, and don't forget to add additional herbs and spices if you have them. It's important to look at the flavors in your salad bowl as a whole when deciding on a dressing: If bitter flavors dominate, balance them out with a sweeter vinaigrette or additional candied nuts or sweet fruits. If your salad tastes mild, a flavorful dressing is probably the right choice. Just make sure to not drown your salad in the dressing – a few tablespoons are typically enough for a few servings.

Toppings

Last but definitely not least, pick something special to top your salad bowl with and make it that much more enjoyable. Add croutons or toasted nuts for more crunch, scatter with mozzarella or feta cheese for added creaminess, sprinkle with chopped herbs for a fresh finish, or top with diced or thinly sliced raw onions for a sharp bite.

Build Your Best Salad Bowl

If you still think salads aren't filling, we hope to convince you otherwise. While there are infinite possibilities for how to assemble a salad bowl, we've made an outline for you to help simplify the process. We've also included our eight favorite recipes for vinaigrettes and dressings to round off your bowl. From simple vinaigrette to creamy ranch dressing, there's an option for everyone, and you'll have a healthy and filling weeknight dinner in no time at all.

(Pseudo-) Grains

Amount: approx. ½ cup (100 g)

- rice
- quinoa
- pearl barley
- spelt

Leafy greens

Amount: approx. 2½ oz (70 g)

- lamb's lettuce
- romaine hearts
- baby spinach
- arugula

Vegetables

Amount: approx. 3 oz (80 g)

- avocado
- cucumber
- sweet potato
- tomato

Protein

Amount: approx. 3½ oz (100 g)

- tofu
- chicken
- salmon
- chickpeas

Vinaigrette and dressing

Amount: approx. ½ cup (120 ml)

- tahini dressing
- yogurt garlic vinaigrette
- balsamic vinaigrette
- herby vinaigrette

Toppings and extras

Amount: to taste

- feta cheese
- red onion
- croutons
- nuts and seeds
- fresh herbs

8 Dressings and Vinaigrettes

Prepare these dressings and vinaigrettes as written or use them as inspiration for your own creations. For the preparation, whisk all ingredients in a bowl until combined or add them to a jar and shake vigorously. Before adding to your salad, season with salt and pepper to taste.

MISO DRESSING
4 tsp toasted sesame oil,
1 tbsp honey,
2 tbsp rice vinegar,
1 minced garlic clove,
2 tsp miso paste,
2 tbsp soy sauce,
1 chopped Thai chili,
¼ oz (5 g) minced ginger

RANCH DRESSING
½ tsp garlic powder,
¼ oz (5 g) chopped chives,
½ cup (120 ml) heavy cream,
1½ oz (40 g) sour cream,
¼ oz (5 g) chopped parsley,
1 cup (200 g) mayonnaise,
2 tbsp lemon juice

HONEY MUSTARD DRESSING
¼ cup (85 g) honey,
¼ cup (60 ml) olive oil,
¼ cup (60 ml) walnut oil,
3 tbsp apple cider vinegar,
¼ cup (60 g) fig mustard

HERBY VINAIGRETTE
3 tbsp olive oil,
1 tbsp red wine vinegar,
1 tbsp dried herbs,
1 chopped garlic clove

CRÈME FRAÎCHE DRESSING
1 tbsp olive oil, 1 tbsp white wine vinegar,
1 tsp sugar, 1 tbsp chopped capers,
1 lemon (juice and zest), 1 chopped garlic clove,
½ oz (10 g) chopped parsley, ¼ oz (5 g) chopped chives,
1 tsp Worcestershire sauce, ¼ oz (5 g) chopped chervil,
¼ cup (60 g) crème fraîche

GARLICKY YOGURT VINAIGRETTE
3 tbsp olive oil,
1 chopped garlic clove,
3 tbsp yogurt,
1 tbsp red wine vinegar

BALSAMIC VINAIGRETTE
1 chopped garlic clove,
1 tbsp balsamic vinegar,
1 tsp mustard,
1 tsp maple syrup,
3 tbsp olive oil

TAHINI DRESSING
¼ oz (5 g) chopped parsley,
1 tbsp lemon juice,
¼ cup (85 g) tahini,
¾ cup (200 g) yogurt,
2 chopped garlic cloves

50 minutes

Crowd-pleaser

Family-friendly

Spinach and white bean soup

"This soup has a special place in my heart. It reminds me of home, although I'm not convinced I ever ate it there. Maybe it's just the combination of comforting flavors in a warm, filling bowl of soup? I can't say for sure, but the point is: This is a cozy, satisfying soup – a whole meal within itself. Serve with crusty bread, if desired."

– Devan

4 servings

9 oz (200 g) spinach
1 red onion
1 carrot
1 stalk celery
5 sun-dried tomatoes
2 cloves garlic
5¼ oz (150 g) Italian
  sausages
chili flakes
1 bay leaf
2 sprigs rosemary
2 sprigs thyme
6 cups (1½ l) vegetable
  broth
7 oz (200 g) canned
  white beans, drained
Parmesan cheese rind
salt
pepper
olive oil for frying

1 Chop spinach. Chop onion, carrot, celery, and sun-dried tomatoes. Peel and mince garlic. Remove sausage meat from the casing and chop roughly.

2 Heat a large pot over medium heat and add enough olive oil to coat the bottom of the pan. Add onion and garlic, and sauté. Add sausage and brown for approx. 15 min. Add carrots, celery, and chili flakes, season with salt and pepper, and let cook for approx. 5 min. more. Add bay leaf, rosemary, thyme, sun-dried tomatoes, vegetable broth, beans, and Parmesan rind, if using. Cover and let simmer until beans are tender, approx. 20 min.

3 Use a fork to gently mash some of the beans. Add spinach and simmer for approx. 10 min. more. Remove bay leaf, rosemary, thyme, and Parmesan rind before serving.

EXTRA TIP
To make this soup vegetarian, simply leave out the Italian sausage and swap in more beans.

25
minutes

Low carb

Summer

Chicken and avocado salad with blueberry vinaigrette

"This salad shines in both flavor and looks, but the highlight of the recipe is definitely the blueberry vinaigrette, which gives the salad a summery, fruity flair. If blueberries aren't in season, you can use thawed, frozen blueberries. You can also swap in fried tofu or shrimp for the chicken."

– Johanna

2 servings

FOR THE SALAD
1 avocado
1 red onion
3 oz (75 g) baby spinach
2 oz (50 g) feta cheese
1 oz (25 g) sliced almonds
10½ oz (300 g) chicken
  breast
2 oz (60 g) blueberries
salt
pepper
olive oil for frying

**FOR THE BLUEBERRY
VINAIGRETTE**
2 oz (60 g) blueberries
¼ cup (60 ml) water
1 tsp honey
1 tsp mustard
2½ tbsp white balsamic
  vinegar
3 tbsp olive oil
salt
pepper

1   Halve avocado, remove pit, and dice. Halve red onion, peel, and slice into thin rings. Add both to a serving bowl with spinach. Crumble in feta.

2   For the vinaigrette, add blueberries, water, and honey to a pot. Let simmer for approx. 5 min. Remove from heat and let cool slightly.

3   Add mustard, white balsamic vinegar, and olive oil to the pot with the blueberries. Use an immersion blender to blend into a smooth dressing and season with salt and pepper.

4   Toast sliced almonds in a frying pan over medium heat for approx. 3 min., or until golden. Remove from heat and set aside. Season chicken breast with salt and pepper. Heat some olive oil in the same pan used to toast the almonds, and fry chicken for approx. 4 min. on either side until cooked through. Remove from heat, let rest briefly, then shred or slice into strips. Add chicken, almonds, and blueberries to the salad bowl and toss with blueberry dressing.

EXTRA TIP
Pitting an avocado doesn't have to be dangerous! See our How-to for an easy and safe way to pit and peel an avocado.

50 minutes

Crowd-pleaser

Family-friendly

Chicken noodle soup

"Chicken noodle soup is a wonderful home remedy if you're feeling a bit under the weather. It warms you up from the inside and even has an anti-inflammatory effect. Even if you're healthy, it's never a bad idea to have some chicken stock in your pantry or freezer. To serve, warm up the stock, boil the noodles in it, and add more water as needed."

– Johanna

6 servings

3½ oz (100 g) bacon
1 onion
7 oz (200 g) potatoes
8½ oz (250 g) carrots
7 oz (200 g) celery
10½ oz (300 g) leeks
1 tbsp butter
1⅓ lb (600 g) chicken legs
2 bay leaves
8½ cups (2 l) vegetable
  broth
7 oz (200 g) dried egg
  noodles
salt
pepper
parsley for serving

1 Cut bacon into small cubes. Peel and mince onion. Peel and dice potatoes and carrots. Dice celery and leeks.

2 Melt butter in a large pot over medium-high heat. Add onion and bacon and fry for approx. 2–3 min. Add chicken legs and fry for approx. 3–5 min. Season with salt and pepper. Add chopped vegetables, bay leaves, and vegetable broth to the pot. Bring to a boil, then cover with a lid and reduce heat to medium. Let simmer for approx. 15 min.

3 Remove chicken from the pot. Set aside and allow to cool. In the meantime, add egg noodles to the pot and cook, covered, for approx. 10 min.

4 Once chicken legs are cool enough to handle, remove the skin and discard. Remove the meat from the bone and cut into bite-size pieces. Add chicken back to the pot. Serve with fresh parsley and season with salt and pepper to taste.

EXTRA TIP
To make this soup ahead, simply prepare everything as written, but cook and store the noodles separately – draining and rinsing them with cold water. When ready to serve, heat everything up together in a pot.

French potato and green bean salad

45
minutes

Vegan

Make
ahead

"I like to serve this salad as a fresh side to grilled dishes, but it also tastes fantastic on its own and will definitely fill you up. Sprinkle it with freshly grated Parmesan cheese for an even more salty, savory (though admittedly not vegan) flavor."

– Johanna

4 servings

2 shallots
1 clove garlic
¼ oz (5 g) parsley
¼ oz (5 g) chives
¼ oz (5 g) chervil
4 tsp white wine vinegar
½ cup (120 ml) vegetable
  broth
1 tbsp mustard
½ cup (120 ml) olive oil
1 lb (500 g) new potatoes
14 oz (400 g) green beans
salt
pepper

1 Mince shallots, garlic, parsley, chives, and chervil. To make the dressing, combine white wine vinegar, vegetable broth, mustard, and olive oil in a bowl. Season with salt and pepper. Add shallots, garlic, and all the chopped herbs and mix well.

2 Add potatoes to a pot with salted water and bring to a boil. Let cook for approx. 20 min., or until cooked through. Blanch green beans for approx. 2 min., then transfer immediately to a large bowl of ice water.

3 Slice potatoes. Trim the ends of the green beans. Mix potatoes and beans with the dressing. Season with salt and pepper.

EXTRA TIP
For more information on how to blanch vegetables, see page 37.

45
minutes

Vegan

Make
ahead

Glass noodle salad with lemongrass dressing

"To be honest, I could eat this salad every day, but it's especially refreshing in the summer, since it's filling but not too heavy. I like to have one serving for dinner and pack the second serving for lunch the next day. The dressing is light enough that the salad can be dressed beforehand, making it easier to pack up."

– Julia

4 servings

1 cucumber
1 carrot
1 yellow bell pepper
1 mango
5¼ oz (150 g) snow peas
9 oz (200 g) glass noodles
2 limes
1 Thai chili
1 stalk lemongrass
2 tbsp sesame oil
2 tbsp soy sauce
2 tsp sugar
2 tsp rice vinegar
½ oz (10 g) mint
½ oz (10 g) cilantro
chopped roasted peanuts
  for garnish
sesame seeds for garnish

1 Halve cucumber width- then lengthwise and slice into half moons. Julienne carrot, bell pepper, and mango into matchsticks.

2 Bring a pot of salted water to a boil. Blanch snow peas for approx. 30 sec. Drain, let cool, and slice diagonally. Cook glass noodles according to the package instructions.

3 Juice limes and thinly slice chili. Tenderize lemongrass by beating the base of it with the back of a knife, then remove the base and fibrous pieces, and thinly slice. In a bowl, combine lemongrass, lime juice, sesame oil, soy sauce, sugar, rice vinegar, and sliced chili. Mix well.

4 Divide glass noodles into serving bowls. Top with sliced vegetables, mango, and lemongrass dressing. Garnish with fresh mint and cilantro, peanuts, and sesame seeds.

EXTRA TIP
This is a perfect salad
for making ahead and
transporting for lunch,
a picnic in the park,
or dinner on the road.
Simply keep the fresh
herbs separate and mix
in just before serving.

5-ingredient sweet potato lentil curry soup

30 minutes

Vegan

Make ahead

"An easy and satisfying soup that comes together quickly, I always prefer to use fresh spinach, but this can also be made with frozen, thawed, and drained spinach. You can try it with regular potatoes instead of sweet and switch up the curry paste depending on what you have on hand."

– Devan

4 servings

1⅓ lb (600 g) sweet potatoes
10½ oz (300 g) baby spinach
1½ tbsp red curry paste
1 cup (240 g) red lentils
1⅔ cups (400 ml) coconut milk
3⅓ cups (800 ml) water
olive oil for sautéing
salt
pepper
yogurt for serving

1 Peel sweet potatoes and cut into bite-size pieces.

2 Drizzle some olive oil into a pot over medium heat. Add sweet potatoes, season with salt and pepper, and sauté for approx. 5 min. Add spinach and cook until wilted. Add red curry paste to the pot and stir to combine. Sauté for approx. 2 min., or until curry paste starts to stick to the bottom of the pot.

3 Add lentils and coconut milk, stirring well to combine. Add water, bring to a simmer, and let cook for approx. 15 min. or until lentils are soft, but not mushy. Serve with yogurt, if desired.

EXTRA TIP

For a different flavor profile, use green or yellow curry paste, regular potatoes, and chopped, mature spinach leaves or kale.

Cauliflower coconut soup
with shrimp

minutes

Low carb

"This creamy soup has everything it needs to convince those who don't like soup and cauliflower skeptics alike with its well-rounded combination of flavors. If you don't have coconut water, you can replace it with regular water."

– Christian

4 servings

FOR THE SOUP

2¼ lb (1 kg) cauliflower
2 cloves garlic
2 onions
1 cup (240 ml) rice wine
2 cups (500 ml) coconut
  water
2 cups (500 ml) coconut
  milk
2 tsp fish sauce
salt
pepper
sugar
vegetable oil for frying

FOR THE SHRIMP

1 clove garlic
2 Thai chilis
4 stalks lemongrass
8 large shrimp, peeled
  and deveined
salt
vegetable oil for frying

1 Remove cauliflower from the stalk and cut into small florets. Peel and roughly chop garlic and onions.

2 Heat some vegetable oil in a pot and sauté cauliflower florets, garlic, and onions for approx. 5 min. Deglaze with rice wine and let simmer for approx. 1–2 min. Add coconut water to the pot and let simmer for approx. 20 min. over medium heat. Then add coconut milk and bring to a boil. Use an immersion blender to blend the soup until smooth. Add fish sauce, and season with salt, pepper, and sugar.

3 To prepare the shrimp, peel and mince remaining garlic. Thinly slice chilis. Slice lemongrass lengthwise into skewers and thread the shrimp onto them. Season shrimp skewers with salt. Heat some vegetable oil in a frying pan and add the shrimp skewers. Flip after approx. 2 min., then add chilis and garlic to sauté alongside the shrimp for approx. 1 min. more. Serve the soup in a bowl and top with the shrimp skewers. Drizzle with some of the chili- and garlic-infused cooking oil.

40
minutes

Low carb

Make
ahead

Cobb salad

"Cobb salad is a classic American salad found all over the country. If you think it looks thrown-together, you'd be right – it's said to have first been made out of leftovers as a midnight snack. As far as we're concerned, that means if you're missing an ingredient we call for here, feel free to swap in whatever you have on hand instead."

– Johanna

2 servings

3½ oz (100 g) bacon
2 eggs
1 tbsp vegetable oil
2 chicken breasts
2 romaine hearts
½ cucumber
1 avocado
5¼ oz (150 g) cherry
  tomatoes
½ red onion
½ oz (10 g) chives
¼ cup (60 ml) olive oil
1½ tbsp balsamic vinegar
1 tsp mustard
2⅔ oz (80 g) blue cheese
salt
pepper

*used Sharon's moist
tender breast recipe
OK, underwhelming
in flavor*

1 Preheat the oven to 325 °F (160 °C). Spread bacon slices on a parchment-lined baking sheet and bake in the oven for approx. 10 min., or until crisp. Boil eggs in a pot of simmering water for approx. 8 min., then remove and cool in a bowl of cold water.

2 Heat vegetable oil in a frying pan over medium heat. Fry chicken breasts on each side for approx. 4 min., or until cooked through. Season with salt and pepper. Remove, let cool for a few minutes, then slice.

3 Slice romaine hearts into strips. Slice cucumber. Halve avocado, remove pit, and slice. Halve cherry tomatoes. Peel red onion and slice into thin rings. Mince chives. Peel and quarter eggs.

4 For the dressing, whisk olive oil, balsamic vinegar, and mustard in a large bowl. Season with salt and pepper. Mix romaine lettuce with the dressing, then arrange on a platter and top with remaining ingredients. Crumble blue cheese on top before serving.

EXTRA TIP
For knife handling tips and tricks, see page 25. To make this salad ahead of time, prepare all the components and store separately until serving.

Creamy zucchini soup

50
minutes

Vegan

Low carb

"Whether it's summer or winter, in my book, creamy soups are always welcome. In this recipe, zucchini meets a little lime, curry, and coconut milk to make this incredibly delicious (vegan!) soup with a unique flavor combination."

– Johanna

4 servings

3 potatoes
3 cloves garlic
⅓ oz (10 g) ginger
1 onion
10 sprigs parsley
2 sprigs mint
1⅓ lb (600 g) zucchini
¼ cup (60 ml)
  vegetable oil
2 tbsp curry powder
½ tsp ground cumin
2½ cups (600 ml)
  vegetable broth
1¼ cups (300 ml)
  coconut milk
salt
pepper
lime juice
curry powder
unsweetened coconut
  flakes for serving
chili flakes for serving
mint for serving

1 Peel and dice potatoes. Mince garlic, ginger, onion, parsley, and mint. Dice zucchini.

2 Heat vegetable oil in a saucepan over medium heat. Sauté garlic, ginger, and onions until golden. Add zucchini and potatoes, season with curry powder, cumin, salt, and pepper, and cook briefly. Pour in vegetable broth and let simmer for approx. 25 min., or until potatoes and zucchini are tender.

3 Remove pan from heat and add coconut milk, chopped parsley, and mint. Blend the soup until creamy and season with salt, pepper, lime juice, and a little more curry powder, if desired. Top with coconut, chili flakes, and fresh mint before serving.

30
minutes

Vegan

Fattoush

"Fattoush is a Lebanese bread salad that's traditionally served as a starter, but in summer it works well as a refreshing and light main. If sumac hasn't made it into your spice rack yet, we'd really recommend picking some up for this recipe. With its sour and bitter notes, it makes a significant contribution and can even be used as a replacement for lemon juice or vinegar in some recipes. If you can't find Persian cucumbers, which are small, thin-skinned, and crisp, you can use English cucumbers instead."

– Julia

4 servings

FOR THE SALAD
14 oz (400 g) Persian
  cucumbers
5⅓ oz (150 g) romaine
  lettuce
10 mixed cherry tomatoes
5 radishes
1 red onion
¾ oz (20 g) parsley
¾ oz (20 g) mint
3 pitas
vegetable oil for frying
sumac for serving

FOR THE DRESSING
1 clove garlic
¼ cup (60 ml) olive oil
1 tsp lemon juice
1 tbsp sumac
½ tsp cinnamon
½ tsp sugar
1 tsp red wine vinegar
salt
pepper

1 Chop Persian cucumbers and romaine lettuce. Halve cherry tomatoes and quarter radishes. Peel, halve, and slice red onion into thin strips. Roughly chop parsley and mint. Add everything to a large bowl and mix.

2 For the dressing, peel and chop garlic. Add olive oil, garlic, lemon juice, sumac, cinnamon, sugar, and red wine vinegar to a small bowl and stir to combine. Season with salt and pepper.

3 Heat vegetable oil in a frying pan and fry pitas on both sides until golden-brown.

4 Add dressing to the salad bowl and toss to coat. Tear crispy pitas into smaller chunks and add to the bowl. Give it a quick mix and serve fattoush with more sumac on top.

EXTRA TIP
No pita bread? Toast
your favorite crusty
bread instead.

minutes

Vegan

Low carb

Carrot miso soup

"Although this carrot soup looks basic, it'll win you over with its flavor. Miso paste provides a savory depth, chili and ginger add a slightly sharp kick, and lime juice brightens the creaminess. If you've made too much, simply freeze the leftovers."

– Julia

4 servings

1 lb (500 g) carrots
1 onion
2 cloves garlic
⅓ oz (10 g) ginger
1 Thai chili
2 tbsp coconut oil
3 cups (750 ml) vegetable
  broth
2½ tbsp white miso paste
1 lime
salt
pepper
coconut milk or cream for
  serving
cilantro for garnish

1 Peel and dice carrots. Chop onion, garlic, ginger, and chili.

2 Heat coconut oil in a large saucepan and sauté onion, garlic, ginger, and chili over medium heat.

3 Add diced carrots and briefly sauté before adding vegetable broth and bringing to a boil. Reduce heat and leave to simmer for approx. 20 min., or until carrots soften slightly.

4 Remove soup from heat and purée with an immersion blender. Return to heat and add miso paste and lime juice. Simmer for 2 min. more. Add a dollop of coconut milk or cream to each bowl, garnish with cilantro, and season with salt and pepper.

EXTRA TIP
This soup can easily be scaled up or down. If you don't have an immersion blender, use a regular countertop blender to purée the soup.

Warm lentil salad with feta cheese

minutes

Vegetarian

From the community

"This recipe, from community member Leonie Schäfer, won the hearts of our test kitchen. The salad comes together quickly, is easy to execute, and tastes great warm or cold. Ras el hanout, a staple spice mix across North Africa, adds an earthy, slightly sweet flavor to the lentils that shouldn't be missed if you can help it."

– Christian

2 servings

4½ oz (125 g) red lentils
1 tbsp ras el hanout
5¼ oz (150 g) lamb's lettuce
2 scallions
3½ oz (100 g) feta cheese
2 tbsp olive oil
1 tbsp balsamic vinegar
salt
pepper

1 Rinse red lentils under running water, then transfer them to a pot and cover with water. Season with salt, pepper, and ras el hanout. Let simmer over medium heat for approx. 10 min., or until tender. Drain and set aside.

2 While lentils cook, wash and dry lamb's lettuce. Thinly slice scallions. Heat half the olive oil in a small frying pan and fry scallions for approx. 2 min.

3 Spread lamb's lettuce on a serving plate and top with cooked lentils. Crumble feta cheese on top using your hands. Add scallions to salad and drizzle with remaining olive oil and balsamic vinegar.

EXTRA TIP
If you don't have red lentils, you can use brown, green, or black ones instead. See page 43 for more information on cooking lentils.

30
minutes

Make
ahead

Pasta salad with parsley pesto

"The parsley pesto is the star of this pasta salad, making it a perfect plus-one to your next barbecue or picnic. You won't need all the pesto for this recipe, so store the rest in the fridge for later. It'll taste even better after sitting in the fridge for a day. Feel free to swap in almonds or walnuts instead of hazelnuts."

– Jost

4 servings

FOR THE PARSLEY PESTO
3½ oz (100 g) hazelnuts
1 clove garlic
1 oz (25 g) parsley
½ tsp sea salt
6 tbsp olive oil
2 oz (60 g) grated
  Parmesan cheese
½ lemon

FOR THE PASTA SALAD
1 yellow bell pepper
½ tsp sugar
10½ oz (300 g) farfalle
3½ oz (100 g) sun-dried
  tomatoes
2 oz (60 g) pine nuts
2 oz (60 g) grated
  Parmesan cheese
salt
pepper
parsley for serving
olive oil for serving

1 For the pesto, chop hazelnuts, peel garlic, and pluck parsley leaves from the stems. Add parsley leaves, sea salt, and garlic to a food processor and blend. Add olive oil and continue blending until smooth. Stir in Parmesan cheese and chopped hazelnuts, and finish with the juice of half a lemon. Set aside.

2 Core and dice bell pepper. Heat a frying pan over medium heat. Add peppers and sugar, letting them caramelize for approx. 5 min. Season with pepper, wipe out pan, and set bell peppers aside.

3 Bring a large pot of salted water to a boil. Add pasta and cook until al dente, or according to the package instructions. Chop sun-dried tomatoes and toast pine nuts in the same pan you fried the bell pepper in until golden-brown.

4 Drain pasta and rinse under cold water, then transfer to a large bowl. Add caramelized bell peppers, sun-dried tomatoes, and parsley pesto. Toss to combine. Season with salt and pepper and sprinkle with toasted pine nuts and remaining Parmesan cheese. Top with fresh parsley and a drizzle of olive oil, if desired.

EXTRA TIP
If you already have a mortar and pestle, this pesto is the perfect opportunity to put it to use.

Vegetarian
& Vegan

Weeknight chickpea dal

30 minutes

Vegan

Crowd-pleaser

"A quick dal is a true weeknight hero. It can be built entirely from pantry ingredients but can also make a great base for fresh vegetables – or, in this case, fruit. Green apple lends sweetness and acidity to this dish. I always make extra so I can take leftovers to work – the time sitting in the fridge only serves to deepen the flavors.

Although this is a time-saving weeknight recipe, I still like to add some colorful garnishes at the end, like quick-pickled red onions, fresh cilantro, and a splash of coconut milk, to make the dish feel a bit more exciting – because why not make the midweek a little fancy?"

– Ruby

4 servings

FOR THE DAL
1 red onion
1 Granny Smith apple
3 cloves garlic
½ oz (15 g) ginger
2 cardamom pods
2 tbsp coconut oil
2 tsp ground coriander
1 tsp turmeric
½ tsp smoked paprika
½ tsp chili flakes
28 oz (800 g) canned
  chickpeas, drained
1 cup (240 ml) water
1 cup (240 ml) coconut milk
½ lime
cilantro for serving
basmati rice for serving

**FOR THE QUICK-PICKLED
ONIONS**
1 red onion
1 lime

1 Peel and mince red onion, then set aside. Roughly grate the apple and finely grate garlic and ginger. Crush cardamom pods with the back of your knife.

2 For the quick-pickled onions, peel and thinly slice red onion. Add to a bowl along with lime juice. Pour hot water over the mixture until sliced onions are just covered. Let sit until serving.

3 Melt coconut oil in a frying pan over medium-low heat. Add diced red onion and fry for approx. 5 min., or until translucent and softened. Add grated garlic, ginger, coriander, turmeric, smoked paprika, chili flakes, and crushed cardamom pods. Fry for approx. 1 min., or until fragrant.

4 Add grated apple and chickpeas and stir to combine. Deglaze with water and bring to a boil. Let the mixture simmer for approx. 5 min., then reduce the heat to medium-low and let simmer for approx. 10 min. Use a cooking spoon to mash about one-fourth of the chickpea mixture in the pot. Add coconut milk and the juice of half of a lime. Remove cardamom pods before serving. Serve dal with basmati rice and remaining lime on the side. Top dal with a dollop of coconut milk, quick-pickled onions, and cilantro.

EXTRA TIP
Best served with hot basmati rice. See more details on how to cook rice on page 42. This dish can also easily be scaled up or down.

For Quick, Veg-Forward Curries – Look to the Pantry!

Curry? You can indeed make it in a hurry. In only 30 minutes, you can create a filling and delicious curry that'll taste even better the next day. The following ideas are inspired by taste combinations with origins from across the Indian subcontinent through to Southeast Asia. Here are the key pillars to work with when improvising.

The spices to have on hand

You can of course use a pre-mixed curry powder of your choice to create the base flavor. To this, I like to add extra enhancements to dial up certain notes, such as a cinnamon stick or a couple of crushed cardamom pods. For convenience, you can keep ground spices, but make sure not to keep them too long as their flavors will dull over time.

If you have a mortar and pestle, purchase whole spices, which tend to be more flavorful, and use them whole when a recipe calls for it, or grind them yourself. To always be curry-ready, keep the following on hand: cumin, coriander (whole seeds or ground), garam masala, smoked paprika, cinnamon sticks, chili powder, cardamom pods, all-purpose curry powder, and turmeric. Keep spice pastes like green or red curry paste in the fridge, or make your own by blending dried spices with an immersion blender.

Bloom before you begin

Whether the base of your curry is dry (comprised of dry spices, plus alliums like onion, garlic, and ginger) or made with a wetter spice paste (made from scratch or store-bought), it's important to sauté these mixtures over medium-low heat until fragrant, which will help to release the flavors – a process called "blooming."

The pulses to keep in your pantry

Dried beans like black beans and chickpeas, or hearty lentils with a shell such as brown lentils and urad dal, are best soaked overnight. This will not only lead to a faster cooking time, but makes them easier to digest. Bring the soaked pulses to a boil in a large pot of salted water and cook for approx. 15 min., or until softened, then drain and use in your recipe. Red and yellow lentils can be used straight away, as can many canned pulses.

The vegetables

Almost any vegetable will work in a veg-forward weeknight curry – think sweet potato, potato, carrot, cauliflower, broccoli, beans, eggplant, pumpkin, and spinach. Just make sure to add heartier vegetables to your pot first, and softer, leafy greens or veg later, to make sure your textures are intact.

Additional flavorings

There are many ways to add even more flavors and textures to your curries. To make a creamy curry, add coconut milk, heavy cream, or yogurt when the curry is almost done cooking. For sweetness and acidity, add a couple of teaspoons of tomato paste just after you fry your onions, ginger, and garlic – cook until the paste begins to darken and caramelize, which will add richer color and flavor. For something fresher, grate in a green apple as we do in our chickpea dal. If you're aiming for a Southeast Asian-inspired curry, add fish sauce for umami or lime juice for tanginess.

Final tip

You can't deny that a curry intensifies with time, and the trick with speedy curries is to not serve them piping hot. Let them rest for 5 minutes before serving, which will allow you to taste all the intricate flavors better.

Curry in a Hurry!
3 Weeknight Curry Combos

Use this infographic to build easy weeknight curries. All curries start with step 1, the must-have basis for your curry: Sauté garlic, onion, and ginger in ghee or oil. In step 2, choose a flavor profile for your curry and add these ingredients to your softened alliums, and fry until fragrant, approx. 1 min. In step 3, choose the main protein for your curry. Add this to your pot along with the vegetable options given in step 4. In step 5, choose your liquids. Simmer until the curry is cooked and choose your final garnishes in step 6.

Serves 4

1
START WITH

garlic

onion

ginger

2
CHOOSE YOUR SPICE BASE

Spicy

2 tsp ground coriander

2 tsp garam masala

1 tsp turmeric

½ tsp chili powder

Sweet and spicy

1 tbsp curry powder

1 tsp turmeric

1 cinnamon stick

2 cardamom pods

2 cloves

Bright

4 tbsp ground coriander

1 tbsp fish sauce

1 tsp ground turmeric

1 stalk lemongrass

1 green chili

1 lime (zest)

Rich

1 tbsp garam masala

1 tsp whole cumin seeds

1 tsp smoked paprika

2 tbsp tomato paste

3	**4**	**5**	**6**
CHOOSE YOUR PROTEIN	**ADD YOUR VEGETABLES**	**ADD LIQUID**	**GARNISH**

	a total of 9 oz (250 g)		

9 oz (250 g) dry lentils

green beans

⅓ cup (80 ml) heavy cream / yogurt

red onion

or

sweet potato

or

lime wedges

14 oz (400 g) tofu

eggplant

1 cup (240 ml) coconut milk

Thai chili

or

or

cauliflower

14 oz (400 g) canned crushed tomatoes

toasted coconut flakes

28 oz (800 g) canned black beans

or

+

28 oz (800 g) canned chickpeas

peas, bell peppers, spinach etc.

1 cup (240 ml) water

Add extra water as needed.

fresh cilantro, mint, etc.

Spinach and black bean quesadillas with quick-pickled onions

30 minutes

Vegetarian

Family-friendly

"At its core, a quesadilla is a tortilla filled with cheese and fried. The best thing about them is that you can throw in whatever you have lying around and you'll end up with something crispy on the outside and hot, gooey, and delicious on the inside. Here, the spiced spinach, bean, and cheese filling is perfectly complemented by the bright and tangy pickled onions."

– Steven

4 servings

FOR THE PICKLED ONIONS
2 red onions
¼ tsp salt
1 lime, juiced
1½ tbsp sugar

FOR THE QUESADILLAS
14 oz (400 g) canned black beans
1 clove garlic
½ red bell pepper
2 tsp cumin
2 tsp smoked paprika
2 tsp oregano
2 tsp tomato paste
2 tbsp water
2 oz (60 g) baby spinach
4½ oz (120 g) shredded mozzarella
4½ oz (120 g) shredded cheddar cheese
2 flour tortillas, 8 in. (20 cm) in diameter
salt, pepper
vegetable oil for frying
sour cream for serving
cilantro for garnish

1 For the pickled onions, halve, peel, and thinly slice red onions, then add to a small pot with salt, lime juice, and sugar. Bring to a boil, stirring until the sugar dissolves. Once boiling, continue stirring and simmer for 30 sec., or until the onions are slightly softened, then transfer to a bowl and set aside to cool.

2 Drain and rinse black beans. Mince garlic and chop bell pepper into bite-size pieces. Heat a frying pan with some vegetable oil over medium heat and sauté garlic and pepper for approx. 1 min., then add cumin, smoked paprika, oregano, tomato paste, and water and fry for 1 min. Add spinach and beans and fry until spinach has wilted. Transfer to a large bowl and add shredded mozzarella and cheddar cheeses. Season with salt and pepper, and mix thoroughly.

3 Add the filling to one half of each tortilla and then fold, lightly pressing together to seal the edges. Wipe out the pan you used to fry the vegetables in, and heat some vegetable oil over medium heat. Fry two folded tortillas at a time for approx. 2 min. on each side, or until golden-brown. Slice into triangles and serve with sour cream, quick-pickled onions, and cilantro.

30 minutes

Vegetarian

Low carb

Red cabbage steaks with ricotta and hazelnut gremolata

"This recipe combines tender red cabbage, creamy ricotta cheese, and a flavorful gremolata made from toasted hazelnuts, garlic, lemon, and fresh parsley. The 'steaks' are a great vegetarian dinner option and only take 30 minutes to prep. If you find yourself with leftover red cabbage, save it to turn into coleslaw."

– Kristin

4 servings

FOR THE RED CABBAGE STEAKS

2 cloves garlic
1 red cabbage
½ lemon, juiced
¼ cup (60 ml) olive oil
9 oz (250 g) ricotta

FOR THE GREMOLATA

1 oz (25 g) parsley
2 cloves garlic
1/2 lemon
2 oz (50 g) hazelnuts
¾ cup (185 ml) olive oil
salt
pepper

1 For the red cabbage steaks, preheat the oven to 350 °F (180 °C). Peel and mince garlic. Cut red cabbage into approx. ¾–1¼ in. (2–3 cm) thick slices. Transfer to a parchment-lined baking sheet.

2 Add olive oil to a small bowl, along with lemon juice and half the minced garlic. Stir to combine and season with salt and pepper to taste. Brush red cabbage slices with garlic-oil mixture. Bake at 350 °F (180 °C) for approx. 20 min., or until cooked through.

3 For the gremolata, mince parsley, peel and mince garlic, and zest and juice lemon. Toast hazelnuts in a frying pan over medium-high heat. Remove from heat, let cool, and roughly chop. Add hazelnuts to a bowl with parsley, chopped hazelnuts, garlic, lemon zest, lemon juice, and olive oil. Stir to combine and season gremolata with salt and pepper to taste.

4 Remove roasted red cabbage steaks from the oven and top with ricotta and hazelnut gremolata before serving.

Djuvec rice

"Djuvec is a rice dish from Southeast Europe (think Bosnia, Serbia, and Croatia). There's no standard recipe, so there are several regional variations – some vegetarian, some with meat – but what do all the recipes have in common? They only require one pan! If you can't find ajvar, you can make it from scratch or use harissa paste in a pinch."

– Christian

30

minutes

Vegan

Family-
friendly

4 servings

1 onion
1 clove garlic
1 carrot
1 red bell pepper
1 oz (25 g) parsley
2 tbsp vegetable oil
10½ oz (300 g) basmati
  rice
2 cups (500 ml)
  vegetable broth
14 oz (400 g) canned
  crushed tomatoes
1 tsp sweet paprika
3½ oz (100 g) ajvar
10¾ oz (300 g) frozen
  peas
salt
pepper

1 Peel and mince onion, garlic, and carrot. Core and dice bell pepper, then mince parsley and set aside.

2 Heat vegetable oil in a deep frying pan over medium heat. Add onion, garlic, carrot, and bell pepper. Fry for approx. 5 min. Stir in rice and let fry for 1 min. more.

3 Add vegetable broth, canned crushed tomatoes, paprika, ajvar, and frozen peas. Season with salt and pepper, bring to a boil, and let simmer uncovered for approx. 20–25 min., stirring from time to time. Before serving, stir in parsley and season again with salt and pepper.

60 minutes

Vegetarian

Crowd-pleaser

Leek and mushroom tart

"This tart is not only a delicious savory bake, but a real eye-catcher. To get the right texture for the dough, it's important that all the ingredients are cold and that you chill the dough thoroughly before rolling it out. To blind bake the crust, you can use pie weights, or even dried peas, lentils, or rice."

– Johanna

8 servings

FOR THE DOUGH
7 oz (200 g) flour
1 egg, cold
4½ oz (125 g) butter, cold
¼ tsp salt
1 tsp herbes de Provence
¼ cup (60 ml) water, cold

FOR THE FILLING
4 leeks
10½ oz (300 g) king oyster
  mushrooms
1¼ oz (40 g) Gruyère
  cheese
2 tbsp olive oil
1 cup (240 ml) heavy cream
3 eggs
3½ oz (100 g) crème
  fraîche
salt
pepper
nutmeg

1 For the dough, pile flour on a work surface and form a hollow in the middle. Crack egg directly into the hollow and whisk with a fork. Dice cold butter and add to the flour mixture, along with the salt and herbes de Provence. Use a pastry cutter (or your hands) to incorporate all ingredients until the pieces of butter are about the size of a pea. Little by little, add cold water and knead gently to form a cohesive dough. Cover with plastic wrap and refrigerate for approx. 20 min.

2 In the meantime, for the filling, halve leeks lengthwise and wash thoroughly. Dice king oyster mushrooms and grate Gruyère cheese. Heat olive oil in a frying pan over medium heat. Add king oyster mushrooms and fry for approx. 4–5 min., or until golden-brown. In a bowl, mix heavy cream, eggs, grated Gruyère, and crème fraîche, and season with salt, pepper, and freshly grated nutmeg. Add fried mushrooms to the mixture and stir to combine.

3 Preheat the oven to 350°F (180°C). Roll out dough until it's approx. ¾ in. (2 cm) wider than the bottom of the baking pan (8.5 × 12 in. [20 × 30 cm] with a removable bottom). Transfer dough to the pan and carefully push the dough to go up the sides of the pan approx. ¾ in. (2 cm). Prick dough with a fork several times, then place a sheet of parchment paper on the crust and fill it with pie weights. Bake crust for approx. 10 min., then remove pie weights and parchment paper and bake for another 5 min.

4 Remove tart pan from the oven and fill crust with mushroom-cheese mixture. Spread halved leeks, cut-side up, over the top. Bake for approx. 20 min.

Mushroom Stroganoff with crispy potato rösti

30
minutes

Vegetarian

Crowd-pleaser

"For this vegetarian dish, inspired by the Russian classic beef Stroganoff, I used a mixture of button and king oyster mushrooms. The latter hold up really well to heat, which makes them a great choice for a hearty stew like this. If you can't find them or don't like how they taste, use more button mushrooms instead."

– Christian

4 servings

1 onion
2 cloves garlic
4 pickles
1 red beet, cooked
9 oz (250 g) button mushrooms
9 oz (250 g) king oyster mushrooms
2 tbsp tomato paste
2 tbsp vodka
¼ cup (60 ml) white wine
1½ cup (350 ml) vegetable broth
1 tbsp cornstarch
1 tbsp water
18 oz (600 g) floury potatoes
salt
pepper
nutmeg
vegetable oil for frying
sour cream for serving
parsley for serving

1 Peel and thinly slice onion and garlic. Slice pickles and red beet. Halve button mushrooms and chop king oyster mushrooms.

2 Heat vegetable oil in a large frying pan over medium heat. Add mushrooms and fry for approx. 3–4 min. Add onion and garlic and keep frying for approx. 5 min., or until onions are translucent. Whisk in tomato paste, vodka, and white wine, then let the mixture simmer for approx. 5 min. Add vegetable broth, red beet, and pickles. Bring to a boil. In a small bowl, whisk cornstarch and water, then add mixture to the frying pan. Let simmer for approx. 10 min. and season with salt and pepper to taste.

3 While Stroganoff simmers, peel and grate potatoes. Add to a bowl and season with salt, pepper, and freshly grated nutmeg. Use a clean kitchen towel to help you squeeze out as much liquid as possible from grated potatoes. In a separate frying pan, heat vegetable oil over medium heat. Add spoonfuls of potato mixture and fry on both sides until golden-brown. Serve mushroom Stroganoff with crispy potato rösti, sour cream, and parsley.

40
minutes

Vegan

Crowd-
pleaser

Spicy chickpea burgers

"A veggie burger's success often boils down to two factors: having flavors that can stand on their own next to the toppings, sauces, and buns you serve it with (they're half the fun of burger-eating, anyway), and texture. Here, a blend of chickpeas, walnuts, and rice make for a hearty, savory bite, while bold herbs and spices pack a punch. If your food processor is on the small side, blend everything together in batches for the best result."

– Julie

8 servings

5⅓ oz (150 g) basmati rice
2 shallots
4¼ oz (120 g) walnuts
1 tbsp paprika
3 tbsp chili powder
1 tbsp ground cumin
1 oz (20 g) cilantro
¼ cup (60 ml) olive oil
1⅓ oz (40 g) panko
  breadcrumbs
1 tbsp tomato paste
14 oz (400 g) canned
  chickpeas, drained
2 oz (65 g) ketchup
3½ oz (100 g) vegan
  mayonnaise
½ tsp hot sauce
2 tomatoes
½ cucumber
8 burger buns
8 leaves lettuce
salt
pepper
vegetable oil for frying

EXTRA TIP
Use a grill pan for a
true barbecue feel, or
swap it for a frying pan
if you don't have one.
The leftover patties also
freeze well for a future
on-demand meal.

1 Cook basmati rice in a pot, according to the package instructions. In the meantime, peel and mince shallots. Heat vegetable oil in a frying pan over medium heat. Fry shallots for approx. 2–3 min., or until translucent. In another frying pan over medium heat, toast walnuts for approx. 3–5 min. Remove from the pan and let cool.

2 Add cooled walnuts, paprika, chili powder, ground cumin, salt, and pepper to a food processor and blend until the mixture is finely ground.

3 Add cooked rice, shallots, cilantro, olive oil, panko breadcrumbs, tomato paste, and chickpeas to the food processor. Pulse until combined, but not smooth, to retain a bit of texture. Season with salt and pepper to taste.

4 Form the mixture into 8 burger patties. Heat a grill pan over medium heat and coat lightly with oil. When hot, grill burger patties for approx. 5 min. per side.

5 In the meantime, mix ketchup, mayonnaise, and hot sauce in a bowl and set aside.

6 Thinly slice tomatoes and cucumber. Halve burger buns and toast them, if desired. Spread a layer of burger sauce on each half and top with lettuce, a chickpea patty, cucumber, and tomato.

45

minutes

Vegan

Winter

Crispy roasted Brussels sprouts with soy sauce and rice

"Brussels sprouts may not be everyone's cup of tea, but this recipe has managed to convince everyone who's tried it. Its sweetness harmonizes perfectly with the umami-packed soy sauce marinade. Although I use chili paste (harissa or sambal oelek would both do well here) and dried chilis, the dish isn't overly spicy."

– Johanna

6 servings

2¼ lb (1 kg) Brussels sprouts
¼ cup (60 ml) toasted sesame oil
9 oz (250 g) basmati rice
2 cloves garlic
⅓ oz (10 g) ginger
2 dried red chilis
4 sprigs mint
2 tbsp sesame seeds
1 tsp chili paste
2 tbsp sugar
⅓ cup (75 ml) soy sauce
¼ cup (60 ml) mirin
2 tbsp rice wine vinegar
salt
toasted sesame oil for frying

1 Preheat oven to 425°F (220°C). Halve Brussels sprouts and add to a bowl. Add toasted sesame oil, season with salt, and stir to combine. Transfer to a baking sheet and bake for approx. 20 min.

2 In the meantime, cook basmati rice according to the package instructions. Peel and mince garlic and ginger. Mince dried chilis and julienne mint. Toast sesame seeds in a frying pan until fragrant and golden-brown.

3 Heat some sesame oil in a small pot. Add ginger and garlic and fry over medium heat for approx. 2–3 min. Add chili paste and fry for approx. 2 min. Add dried chilis, sugar, soy sauce, mirin, and rice wine vinegar and let simmer until the mixture thickens. Remove from heat and let cool.

4 Add roasted Brussels sprouts and soy sauce marinade to a large bowl and toss to coat. Sprinkle with toasted sesame seeds and mint, and serve with basmati rice.

EXTRA TIP
This dish can easily be scaled up or down. For more on roasting vegetables, see page 29.

Pumpkin and tofu summer rolls with two dipping sauces

30 minutes

Vegan

From the community

"Everyone loves traditional Vietnamese summer rolls, and this seasonal adaptation from our community member Mareike Lambertz, who blogs at 'Vegold,' is no exception. If pumpkin isn't in season, just replace it with more red cabbage, cucumber, or tofu."

– Christian

2 servings

FOR THE SUMMER ROLLS
5⅓ oz (150 g) red cabbage
½ cucumber
4 sprigs mint
7 oz (200 g) glass noodles
10⅔ oz (300 g) Hokkaido pumpkin
7 oz (200 g) tofu
10 rice paper wrappers
vegetable oil for frying

FOR THE SOY DIP
1 clove garlic
1 tbsp vegetable oil
1 tbsp sugar
2 tbsp soy sauce
1 tbsp hoisin sauce

FOR THE PEANUT DIP
1 tbsp soy sauce
1 tbsp tahini
2 tbsp peanut butter
5 tbsp water

1 Slice red cabbage into thin strips. Halve cucumber lengthwise, remove seeds, and cut into thin strips. Remove leaves from mint sprigs. Cook glass noodles according to the package instructions and drain well. Cut pumpkin into strips. Chop tofu and pat dry on both sides with paper towels. For the peanut dip, mix soy sauce, tahini, peanut butter, and water together until smooth.

2 Add pumpkin to a frying pan with some vegetable oil, let cook until tender, then remove and set aside. Add more vegetable oil to the pan and fry tofu until crisp. Dab pumpkin and tofu dry with a paper towel to remove any excess oil. For the soy dip, peel and mince garlic. Add vegetable oil to a pan with garlic and sugar and let caramelize. Deglaze with soy sauce and hoisin sauce and remove from heat.

3 Fill a wide container with cold water and submerge one rice paper wrapper completely. Be careful not to fold or bend it. Spread the wet rice paper wrapper flat on a damp kitchen towel. Arrange filling ingredients horizontally in the middle, leaving approx. ¾ in. (2 cm) of rice paper wrapper at the left and right ends. Fold the left and right ends in, then roll up everything from bottom to top, using the kitchen towel to help you. Serve the summer rolls with the two dipping sauces.

30

minutes

Vegan

Crowd-
pleaser

Sweet potato and bean chili

"As much as I like to eat vegan chili, I don't like it when it only contains canned beans and tomatoes. That's why this recipe features sweet potato and quinoa to add some extra texture and warm flavor. My secret for this recipe are the walnuts, which add a crunchy bite to mix up the softer textures."

– Julia

4 servings

5¼ oz (150 g) quinoa
1 sweet potato
1 bell pepper
1 onion
2 cloves garlic
7 oz (200 g) canned black
  beans
7 oz (200 g) canned kidney
  beans
3½ oz (100 g) canned corn
2 oz (50 g) walnuts
1 tsp chili powder
½ tsp smoked paprika
½ tsp cayenne pepper
1 tsp ground cumin
1 tbsp dried oregano
28 oz (800 g) canned
  crushed tomatoes
1 cup (240 ml) vegetable
  broth
1 tbsp soy sauce
2 tbsp cane sugar
1 avocado
salt
pepper
lime juice
vegetable oil for frying
cilantro for serving
plant-based yogurt for
  serving

1 Rinse quinoa in a sieve under cold water and set aside.
   Peel sweet potato and onion, then dice along with the bell
   pepper. Peel and mince garlic. Drain and rinse black beans,
   kidney beans, and corn. Roughly chop walnuts.

2 Heat vegetable oil in a pot over medium-high heat and fry
   onion, garlic, sweet potato, and bell pepper for approx.
   3 min. Add chili powder, paprika, cayenne pepper, cumin,
   and oregano to the pot and mix well. Sauté for approx.
   4–5 min.

3 Add crushed tomatoes, vegetable broth, and quinoa to the
   pot. Season with soy sauce, cane sugar, salt, and pepper.
   Bring to a boil and let cook, covered, for approx. 15–20 min.
   During the last 5 min., add black beans, kidney beans, corn,
   and walnuts to the pot.

4 Halve, pit, and dice avocado. Season the chili with salt,
   pepper, and lime juice to taste. Serve with chopped cilantro,
   avocado, and a dollop of plant-based yogurt.

EXTRA TIP
This dish can easily be
scaled up or down. Store
leftovers in the fridge for
2–3 days or freeze for up
to 2 months.

5-ingredient beet risotto

35 minutes

Vegetarian

"This risotto is a no-fuss recipe. Feel free to enrich the broth with a Parmesan rind (not vegetarian or vegan!), bay leaf, spare carrots, or celery. If you like, you can add chopped, cooked red beets when you add the rice. For a non-vegetarian version, add a generous amount of Parmesan cheese when you add the butter to the finished risotto."

– Ruby

2 servings

1 onion
3 cups (750 ml)
  vegetable broth
1½ cups (360 ml) beet
  juice, divided
9 oz (250 g) risotto rice
⅓ cup (80 ml) white
  wine
salt
pepper
olive oil for frying
butter for serving

1 Peel and mince onion. Heat up vegetable broth and 1 cup (240 ml) beet juice in a pot. In another pot, heat a generous amount of olive oil over medium-low heat. Add onion and sauté until soft and translucent, approx. 6 min. Add risotto rice and fry for approx. 2 min.

2 Deglaze onions and rice with white wine, and stir until fully absorbed. Add warmed vegetable broth and beet juice to the rice, one ladleful at a time, stirring constantly between each addition, until the liquid is fully absorbed. Repeat this process until the rice is al dente and the mixture creamy.

3 Stir in remaining ½ cup (120 ml) beet juice and season with salt and pepper. Stir a knob of butter through the risotto before serving.

EXTRA TIP
Make this risotto vegan by leaving the butter out. Garnish with vegetarian Parmesan or nutritional yeast if desired.

60
minutes

Vegan

Make
ahead

Vegan spinach and mushroom lasagna

"Kicking the dairy out of a lasagna recipe is a risky business, and skeptics are sure to say it's not a good idea. But this recipe has omnivores (including myself) convinced that with a few smart substitutions and a well-rounded foundation of flavor, you don't even miss the cheese. Skip the nutritional yeast if you can't find it, though it does add a nice Parmesan-esque oomph to the vegan béchamel sauce."

– Julie

8 servings

1 onion
2 cloves garlic
14 oz (400 g) button
  mushrooms
8 sprigs thyme
½ cup (100 g) margarine
3 tbsp flour
2 cups (500 ml) soy milk,
  warm
2 tbsp nutritional yeast
1 tsp ground nutmeg
5¼ oz (150 g) spinach
2 cups (500 g) tomato
  purée
8 oz (250 g) lasagna
  noodles
salt
pepper
olive oil for frying and
  greasing

1 Peel and mince onion and garlic. Clean and slice mushrooms. Pluck thyme leaves from sprigs.

2 Melt margarine in a saucepan over medium heat. Whisk in flour, then slowly whisk in warm soy milk in a steady stream. Season the vegan béchamel with nutritional yeast, ground nutmeg, salt, and pepper to taste.

3 Heat olive oil in a frying pan over medium heat. Sauté onion and garlic for approx. 2–3 min., or until translucent. Add mushrooms and half the thyme leaves and cook for approx. 5 min., or until mushrooms start to brown. Add spinach and cook until wilted. Season the vegetable mixture with salt and pepper and set aside.

4 Preheat the oven to 400 °F (200 °C). Grease a baking dish with some olive oil. Start with a layer of tomato purée on the bottom, then add a layer of lasagna noodles. Spread some more tomato purée on top, followed by a layer of vegetables and a layer of béchamel. Top with another layer of lasagna noodles and repeat the step until all ingredients are used up. Finish with a layer of béchamel and sprinkle with remaining thyme leaves. Bake for approx. 30 min., or until golden-brown. Let cool slightly before slicing and serving.

EXTRA TIP
Layer the lasagna up to one day ahead and store in the fridge before baking the next day.

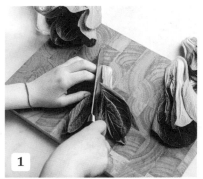

Bok choy and crispy tofu stir-fry

"If you're not a fan of tofu yet, this recipe is here to convince you otherwise. Tossing tofu in cornstarch ensures the edges crisp up perfectly when fried for an irresistible texture. It's served here with rice, but rice noodles make another great pairing if you prefer them."

– Johanna

2 servings

4½ oz (125 g) basmati rice

1 scallion

3 cloves garlic

1 Thai chili

4 heads bok choy

2 tbsp rice wine

2 tbsp soy sauce

2 tbsp water

1 tbsp brown sugar

10½ oz (300 g) tofu

2 tbsp cornstarch

½ tsp salt

3 tbsp toasted sesame oil

1 Cook basmati rice in a pot, according to the package instructions. In the meantime, peel and mince scallion and garlic. Deseed chili and slice into thin rings. Trim the ends off bok choy heads and slice each lengthwise into strips. For the sauce, mix rice wine, soy sauce, water, and brown sugar in a small bowl.

2 Pat tofu dry on all sides, then dice into bite-size pieces. Add to a bowl with cornstarch and salt and toss to coat.

3 Heat toasted sesame oil in a frying pan over medium heat. Add tofu and sear for approx. 3–5 min., or until crisp. Remove from the pan and drain on paper towels. Add bok choy, scallion, garlic, and chili to the same frying pan and sauté for approx. 2–3 min., then deglaze with sauce. Transfer crispy tofu back to the pan and toss to combine. Serve with cooked basmati rice.

EXTRA TIP
Serve with rice or rice noodles. For more details on how to cook these pantry staples, see pages 42–43.

40

minutes

Vegetarian

Sweet potato fritters with guacamole and poached eggs

"Breakfast for dinner is never a bad idea, especially if these sweet potato fritters are involved. If you don't have sweet potatoes around, use regular, floury potatoes instead. To poach the eggs one-by-one, add them to a bowl of cold water after fishing them out of the pot, which will stop the cooking process and ensure a runny yolk."

– Christian

4 servings

FOR THE SWEET POTATO FRITTERS
1⅓ lb (600 g) sweet
  potatoes
2 cloves garlic
5 tbsp olive oil
3 eggs
1 tsp ground coriander
1 tsp ground caraway
6 tbsp cornstarch
salt
pepper
vegetable oil for frying

FOR THE GUACAMOLE
½ oz (10 g) cilantro
2 tomatoes
2 avocados
1 lime
1 tbsp sugar
1½ tsp chili flakes
salt
pepper

FOR THE POACHED EGGS
2 tsp distilled white
  vinegar
4 eggs

1 For the sweet potato fritters, peel sweet potatoes and grate with a box grater. Place grated sweet potato into a kitchen towel, wrap, and squeeze well to remove any excess water. Transfer to a bowl. Mince garlic and add to bowl with sweet potatoes. Add olive oil, eggs, ground coriander, ground caraway, salt, and pepper, and mix well. Add cornstarch and mix again just to combine.

2 For the guacamole, chop cilantro and set aside. Quarter tomatoes, remove seeds, and chop into small pieces. Halve avocados and remove pits. Add avocado flesh to a liquid measuring cup and purée with an immersion blender. Add lime juice, sugar, and chili flakes, and stir to combine. Season with salt and pepper to taste. Stir tomatoes and cilantro through the guacamole.

3 Heat vegetable oil in a large frying pan. Add in spoonfuls of sweet potato mixture and fry in batches, pressing them flat, and frying on both sides until golden-brown. Remove from pan and let cool on paper towels.

4 For the poached eggs, bring a small saucepan of water to a simmer and add vinegar. Crack each egg into a small bowl and release into the water by gently lowering the bowl to touch the surface of the water. Remove after approx. 2 min. for a soft egg or approx. 4 min. for a firm egg. Serve sweet potato fritters with guacamole and poached eggs.

EXTRA TIP
Craving more instructions on poaching a perfect egg? See our How-to here.

1

2

3

4

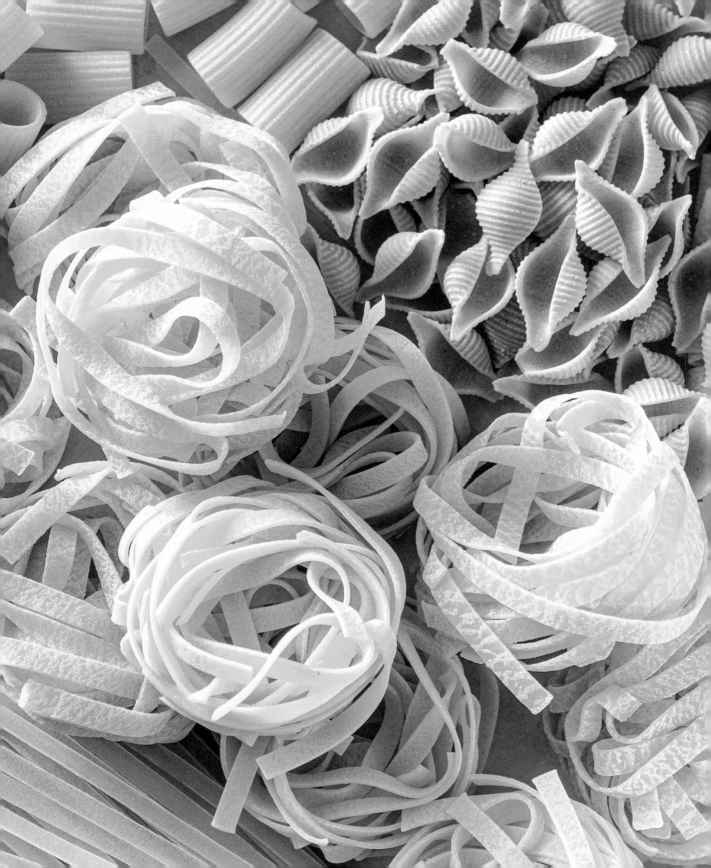

Pasta &
Noodles

Rigatoni with walnut-ricotta pesto

30
minutes

Make ahead

Crowd-pleaser

"Pasta and pesto are an ideal team, and they're a classic go-to for an effortless dinner after a long day. The best thing about this match? You can vary the types of pastas and pestos to suit your mood and keep things fresh in the kitchen. If you feel a bit lost when it comes to combining different herbs, nuts, and aromatics in your pestos, don't fret – you'll find plenty of inspiration on the following pages!

We chose to showcase a pesto variation that combines the intense nuttiness of roasted walnuts with creamy ricotta and fresh, bracing bites of parsley and lemon. It's a uniquely delicious pesto, the likes of which we're sure you've never tasted before."

– Kristin

4 servings

FOR THE PASTA AND PESTO
3½ oz (100 g) walnuts,
  toasted
10½ oz (300 g) ricotta
2 oz (50 g) basil
2 cloves garlic
½ lemon, zest and juice
14 oz (400 g) rigatoni
salt
pepper
nutmeg
basil for serving

**FOR THE TOASTED WALNUT
GARNISH**
3 oz (80 g) walnuts
2 anchovies
¼ cup (60 ml) olive oil
1 tsp chili flakes
½ lemon
salt

1 For the pesto, add walnuts, ricotta, basil, peeled garlic cloves, and lemon zest and juice to a food processor and blend until smooth. Season to taste with salt, pepper, and freshly grated nutmeg.

2 Bring a large pot of salted water to a boil. Cook the rigatoni until al dente, or according to the package instructions. Before draining, reserve approx. 1 cup (240 ml) of pasta cooking water and set aside.

3 While the pasta cooks, add the walnuts, anchovies, and olive oil for the toasted walnut garnish to a saucepan. Cook over low to medium heat for approx. 5–6 min., or until walnuts are golden-brown and anchovies have nearly dissolved. Add chili flakes and the juice from the lemon, and season with salt. Mix to combine, then remove from heat.

4 Add approx. 3 tbsp of pasta water to pesto and mix to combine. Toss cooked rigatoni with pesto, adding as much pasta cooking water as necessary for a creamy sauce that sticks to the pasta. Serve with toasted walnut garnish and basil.

EXTRA TIP
For a vegetarian variation,
simply leave out the anchovies.

Pasta & Noodles   155

Why You Should Always Have Pesto On Hand

Whether as an alternative to a classic pasta sauce, dip, spread, or marinade – the possibilities for pesto are nearly endless. The best thing of all? You can easily make all of your favorites at home, so get ready to say goodbye to store-bought pestos for good.

If you asked me which ingredients I couldn't live without, pesto would be high up on my list. My reasons are simple: Pesto stores well, can be adjusted to suit just about anyone's taste, and can boost the flavor of plenty of dishes.

It's also simple to make at any moment and can be whipped up with whichever tool you have at hand, whether that's a food processor, an immersion blender, or a mortar and pestle. To keep it versatile, you can adjust the consistency of any pesto to suit its intended use. The foundation of any pesto is a combination of 5 components: herbs, nuts, cheese, oil, and seasonings. Experimenting with these building blocks will help you find your personal favorites.

The herbs

Leftover, wilting herbs are all the invitation I need to make pesto, but I also love to take inspiration fresh from the market. Basil is the classic choice, but mint, rosemary, sage, cilantro, and other seasonal herbs such as wild garlic make equally wonderful bases. You can also stretch out your herbs by supplementing them with other leafy greens like arugula, kale, or even dandelion greens.

The nuts

Nuts add texture to pesto – so feel free to reach for your favorite kind, whether that's a handful of pine nuts, walnuts, hazelnuts, or almonds. The same applies to sunflower or pumpkin seeds, which offer the same texture but different flavors. Using toasted nuts or seeds will give even more flavor and texture. If you prefer your pesto to be a little chunkier, make it in a mortar and pestle – this will give you more control over the final texture.

The cheese

Aged, hard cheeses like Parmesan or Pecorino are classics for pestos and can also be used in combination with each other, but that's not to say you can't experiment. Try creamy ricotta, Manchego, or, if you don't eat cheese, leave it out entirely. Whichever cheese you choose, it's important to pay attention to the flavor profile of the cheese – saltier kinds may curb the need for extra seasoning in the pesto itself or for a final grating of cheese over the finished dish.

The oil

Oil determines the consistency of your pesto. It's best to add the oil a little at a time, blending or pulsing in between, until you've reached the desired texture. Using more oil will yield a runnier pesto that's perfect for salad dressings or marinades. Using less oil will give you a thicker paste that's better suited for adding to meatballs, spreading on sandwiches, or using as a spread or dip. Whenever you store pesto, it should be covered with a thin layer of oil, which will help preserve it so it can last in the fridge for 2 to 3 weeks.

The choice of oil is up to you. Extra virgin olive oil is the traditional choice for a flavor profile that compliments most pestos, but bolder basil, walnut, or sesame oils can add intrigue if used in small amounts – just make sure to pair these with a neutral oil, like canola, so their flavors aren't overwhelming.

The seasonings

In terms of seasonings, pesto typically doesn't need more than a touch of salt and pepper to taste. However, there's a beloved allium that we'd be remiss not to mention: garlic. Sure, it's not really a seasoning but it adds flavor and "spice" to your pesto. To prevent it from overpowering the other ingredients, start with just one clove or even half a clove – that is, if you choose to add it at all.

More possibilities with pesto

You can also make great pestos with red beets, Swiss chard, pumpkin, sun-dried tomatoes, or even roasted peppers. Take a look at our suggested recipes on the next page, then start experimenting with them yourself!

Cilantro pesto

- 4 oz (100 g) cilantro
- 1 tbsp ginger, minced
- 1 clove garlic
- 3½ tbsp sesame oil
- ½ lemon (juice)
- 1 green chili
- 2 oz (50 g) cashews

White pesto

- 1 clove garlic
- 1½ tbsp olive oil
- 2 oz (50 g) ricotta
- 2 oz (50 g) grated Parmesan cheese
- ½ tsp dried oregano
- 2½ oz (75 g) pine nuts

Walnut-ricotta pesto

- 2½ oz (75 g) walnuts
- 4 oz (100 g) ricotta
- 1 oz (25 g) basil
- 1 clove garlic
- ground nutmeg

Classic basil pesto

- 2 oz (50 g) basil
- 2 oz (50 g) grated Parmesan
- 1 clove garlic
- 3½ tbsp olive oil
- 2 oz (50 g) pine nuts

Wild herb pesto

- 4 oz (100 g) wild herbs
- 2 oz (50 g) grated Pecorino
- 2 oz (50 g) sunflower seeds
- 3 tbsp grapeseed oil
- ½ lemon, juice

Beet pesto

- 1 beet, cooked, peeled, and diced
- 2 oz (60 g) peanuts
- 3 tbsp olive oil
- 1 clove garlic
- ½ lemon, juice
- 1 sprig rosemary, leaves

Arugula-almond pesto

- 4 oz (100 g) arugula
- 1 oz (25 g) almonds
- 2 oz (50 g) grated Parmesan cheese
- ½ oz (15 g) basil
- 1½ tbsp olive oil

Roasted red pepper-hazelnut pesto

- 2 oz (50 g) hazelnuts
- 2 oz (50 g) roasted red peppers
- 2 oz (50 g) grated Parmesan cheese
- 3½ tbsp olive oil
- 1 clove garlic
- ½ oz (15 g) basil

Pistachio pesto

- 2½ oz (75 g) pistachios
- ½ lemon, zest and juice
- 1 clove garlic
- 1 oz (25 g) basil
- ½ oz (15 g) mint
- 5 tbsp olive oil

Tomato-almond pesto

¾ oz (20 g) almonds

2½ oz (75 g) sun-dried tomatoes

sugar

2 oz (50 g) grated Parmesan cheese

1 clove garlic

3½ tbsp olive oil

Dandelion green pesto

2½ oz (75 g) dandelion greens, stems removed

2 oz (50 g) grated Parmesan

1 clove garlic

2 oz (60 g) cashews

3 tbsp olive oil

½ lime, juice

Ginger-beet pesto

1½ tbsp ginger, minced

1 clove garlic

1 tbsp balsamic vinegar

3½ tbsp olive oil

4 oz (100 g) beet, cooked, peeled, and diced

1¾ oz (40 g) pine nuts

Miso-cashew pesto

1 tbsp miso

1 clove garlic

1 lime, zest and juice

2 tbsp mirin

3½ tbsp toasted sesame oil

4½ oz (125 g) cashews

16 Simple Pesto Recipes

Make any of these pestos as written or use them as inspiration for creating your own. Each recipe yields approx. 1 cup (200 g) of pesto. Simply add all the ingredients to a food processor or mortar and pestle, or use an immersion blender to blend until creamy (or chunky – the choice is yours!) Don't forget to season with salt and pepper to taste.

Spiced nut pesto

1¾ oz (40 g) walnuts

1¾ oz (40 g) pine nuts

½ tsp chili powder

5 tbsp olive oil

2 oz (60 g) grated Parmesan cheese

½ clove garlic

1 tbsp mustard

Avocado-kale pesto

4 oz (100 g) kale

1 oz (25 g) pine nuts

3 tbsp olive oil

½ lemon, juice

1 oz (25 g) grated Parmesan cheese

½ avocado, peeled

Sun-dried tomato pesto

4 oz (100 g) sun-dried tomatoes

1 clove garlic

¼ lemon, juice

3½ tbsp olive oil

2 oz (50 g) cashews

25 minutes

Crowd-pleaser

Family-friendly

5-ingredient creamy tomato and basil pasta

"This simple pasta dish uses a generous amount of tomato paste as a base and gets a creamy tang from crème fraîche. You can use heavy cream or mascarpone as a substitute, if desired. When it comes to the type of pasta, I would highly recommend you look out for bucatini, as it's the ideal pasta for slurping up all that sauce."

– Ruby

2 servings

1 red onion
3 cloves garlic
½ cup (100 g) tomato paste
7 oz (200 g) linguine
½ cup (100 g) crème fraîche
salt
pepper
olive oil for frying
grated Parmesan cheese for serving
basil for serving

1 Peel and thinly slice red onion. Crush garlic cloves with the back of a knife, discarding peels.

2 Heat a generous amount of olive oil in a pan over medium heat. Sauté onion and garlic for approx. 2–3 min. Add tomato paste and cook for about 10 min. over low heat, stirring often. In the meantime, bring a pot of water to a boil and season generously with salt. Cook the linguine according to the package instructions. Reserve approx. 1 cup (240 ml) cooking water before draining.

3 Mix half the reserved pasta water with the crème fraîche and pour the mixture into the pan with the tomato paste. Stir to combine and add more pasta water as needed until the simmering sauce is creamy, but not too thick. Season to taste with salt and pepper. Stir in a handful of grated Parmesan cheese, if desired, then add the cooked pasta to the sauce and toss to combine. Serve with basil leaves and more grated Parmesan cheese, if desired.

EXTRA TIP
To make it vegetarian, serve with a sprinkling of nutritional yeast or vegetarian Parmesan cheese.

30 minutes

Crowd-pleaser

Family-friendly

Rigatoni with broccoli and sausage

"Pasta, broccoli, and Italian sausage – it's hard to go wrong with this classic combination. Reusing the starchy cooking water that the broccoli and pasta were cooked in is the secret to this recipe's success, as it allows the oil and Parmesan cheese to bind, stick to the pasta, and form a sauce. You can use any pasta shape you like here; we just prefer rigatoni."

– Johanna

4 servings

1 head broccoli
7 oz (200 g) Italian sausage
1 clove garlic
10½ oz (300 g) rigatoni
¼ cup (60 ml) olive oil
1 tsp chili flakes
1 lemon
1½ oz (40 g) grated
  Parmesan cheese
salt
pepper
basil for serving
grated Parmesan cheese
  for serving

1 Cut broccoli into small florets. Remove the casings from the sausage and roughly chop. Peel and thinly slice garlic.

2 Bring a pot of water to a boil, season generously with salt, and blanch broccoli florets for approx. 3 min. Use a slotted spoon to transfer the broccoli to a bowl of ice water.

3 Cook the rigatoni in the same pot with the same water that you blanched the broccoli in, according to the package instructions. Before draining, reserve ½ cup (120 ml) pasta cooking water and set aside.

4 Heat olive oil in a pan over medium-high heat. Add Italian sausage and garlic and sauté for approx. 4 min. Add blanched broccoli, cooked and drained rigatoni, reserved pasta cooking water, chili flakes, lemon zest and juice, and grated Parmesan cheese. Season with salt and pepper and toss to combine. Serve with basil and more grated Parmesan cheese.

Not
Great

35 minutes

Winter

Orecchiette with creamy Gorgonzola sauce and radicchio

"If you're looking to switch up your typical pasta with tomato sauce, this recipe is for you. The creamy sauce gets a ton of flavor and tang from rich Gorgonzola cheese, and while this combination is often paired with spinach, we opted for bitter radicchio. Depending on the type of Calvados (a type of French apple brandy) you have, it will deepen the flavor of the sauce and add fruity, bittersweet, or even sour notes."

– Christian

4 servings

11 oz (300 g) radicchio
1 oz (25 g) walnuts
11 oz (300 g) orecchiette
2 shallots
1 tsp honey
1 tsp Calvados
¼ cup (60 ml) white wine
¼ cup (60 ml) apple juice
7 oz (200 g) Gorgonzola
  cheese
½ cup (120 ml) heavy
  cream
salt
pepper
nutmeg
olive oil for frying

1 Peel and mince shallots. Quarter radicchio and slice into strips, reserving some quartered leaves. Roughly chop walnuts.

2 Bring a pot of water to a boil and season generously with salt. Cook orecchiette according to the package instructions.

3 In the meantime, heat olive oil in a pan over medium heat, add shallots and sauté for approx. 2 min., or until translucent. Add chopped walnuts and honey and let caramelize over medium-high heat for approx. 3 min., or until walnuts are fragrant and lightly toasted. Add most of the sliced radicchio and sauté for approx. 2 min. more.

4 Deglaze the pan with Calvados, white wine, and apple juice. Break up Gorgonzola, add it to the pan, and let melt. Once melted, add heavy cream and season sauce with salt, pepper, and freshly grated nutmeg. Drain orecchiette, add to sauce, and toss to combine. Serve with remaining radicchio.

Pad see ew (Thai stir-fried noodles)

Family-friendly

"Pad see ew is a popular Thai dish that's bold, salty, savory, and even a bit sweet. Next time you go to a grocery store or specialty shore, keep an eye out for different varieties of soy sauce. This dish marries two very different kinds – Chinese dark and Indonesian sweet – that you should definitely keep stocked in your pantry!"

– Christian

2 servings

11 oz (300 g) rice noodles
¼ oz (10 g) ginger
2 cloves garlic
1 Thai chili
14 oz (400 g) chicken thighs, boneless
5½ oz (150 g) bok choy
¼ cup (60 ml) dark soy sauce
¼ cup (60 ml) sweet soy sauce
2 tbsp oyster sauce
1 tbsp rice vinegar
1 tsp sugar
2 tbsp vegetable oil
2 eggs
toasted sesame oil for serving
sesame seeds for serving

EXTRA TIP
If you have a wok, pull it out for this recipe to make frying and tossing that much easier.

1 Prepare rice noodles according to the package instructions, rinse well with cold water, and set aside. Peel and mince ginger and garlic. Thinly slice chili and chop chicken thighs into bite-size pieces. Use your hands to separate all the individual leaves from the bok choy, then use a knife to separate the stalks from the leaves and halve the stalks lengthwise. In a liquid measuring cup, mix dark and sweet soy sauces with oyster sauce, rice vinegar, and sugar.

2 Heat vegetable oil in a frying pan with a high edge over medium heat. Sauté ginger and garlic, stirring constantly, then add bok choy stems and sauté for approx. 1–2 min. Add chicken and fry for approx. 5 min., then move everything to one side of the pan. Crack eggs into the other side, and scramble vigorously. Before they set completely, add rice noodles and toss everything to combine.

3 Add sauce, chili, and bok choy leaves and fry everything for approx. 2 min. Drizzle pad see ew with toasted sesame oil to taste and sprinkle with sesame seeds before serving.

30
minutes

Make
ahead

Family-
friendly

Spaghetti with lentil Bolognese

"Bolognese sauce is easy to make meatless, as you can swap in mushrooms, cauliflower, or even plant-based ground 'meat,' but this version uses lentils for a savory and quick-cooking sauce that comes together in just 20 minutes. If you have more time, you can let it cook longer to allow the flavors to really develop. This sauce would also be great layered into our vegan spinach and mushroom lasagna on page 140."

– Johanna

4 servings

1 clove garlic
1 onion
1 carrot
2 tbsp olive oil
2 tbsp tomato paste
⅔ cup (150 ml) red wine
1¾ cup (400 ml) vegetable
 broth
2 bay leaves
7 oz (200 g) red lentils
21 oz (600 g) canned
 crushed tomatoes
1 lb (500 g) spaghetti
salt
pepper
sugar
grated Parmesan cheese
 for serving
basil for serving

1 Peel and mince garlic, onion, and carrot.

2 Heat olive oil in a pot over medium heat. Add onions and garlic and sauté for approx. 1 min. Add carrot and fry for approx. 2 min. Add tomato paste and fry for another 2 min. Deglaze with red wine, then add vegetable broth, bay leaves, red lentils, and canned crushed tomatoes. Stir to combine and bring to a simmer. Once simmering, cover and let cook for approx. 20 min.

3 In the meantime, bring a pot of water to a boil and season generously with salt. Cook spaghetti according to the package instructions.

4 Season the Bolognese to taste with sugar, salt, and pepper. Drain spaghetti and add it to the pot with the Bolognese, tossing to combine. Serve with grated Parmesan cheese, if desired, and garnish with basil.

EXTRA TIP
To make this dish vegan or vegetarian, simply serve without the Parmesan cheese. Store any leftover Bolognese in the fridge for 2–3 days, or freeze for up to 2 months.

25

minutes

Family-
friendly

Lemon and hazelnut
spaghetti carbonara

"Spaghetti carbonara is one of my favorite pasta dishes. It can be a bit intimidating, but once you get the technique down, it's easy, and the results are satisfyingly delicious and creamy every time. This version gets a tangy vibrancy from added lemon zest and juice and a nice crunch from toasted hazelnuts. If you love the classic, you have to give this twist a try!"

– Devan

4 servings

3½ oz (100 g) pancetta
2 shallots
4 cloves garlic
1 lemon
2 oz (60 g) Parmesan
  cheese
2 egg yolks
2 oz (50 g) hazelnuts
12 oz (340 g) spaghetti
salt
pepper
olive oil for frying
grated Parmesan cheese
  for serving

1 Dice pancetta. Peel and mince shallots and garlic. Zest lemon and juice half of it. Grate Parmesan cheese and add to a large bowl with egg yolks. Season with salt and pepper and add most of the lemon zest.

2 Toast hazelnuts in a frying pan over medium heat until fragrant, approx. 5 min. Remove from the pan, chop, and set aside.

3 Bring a large pot of water to a boil and season generously with salt. Cook spaghetti according to the package instructions. Reserve about ½ cup (120 ml) of pasta cooking water, then drain.

4 In the meantime, sauté pancetta in olive oil in a large frying pan over medium heat. Once crisp, add garlic and shallots and sauté for approx. 5 min. Season with salt and pepper, then add spaghetti and a quarter of the reserved pasta cooking water. Toss to coat.

5 Transfer spaghetti to the large bowl with Parmesan and egg yolks. Toss well using tongs (or two forks), adding pasta cooking water as needed to create a smooth, glossy sauce that coats the pasta. Add lemon juice and toss some more.

6 Serve spaghetti with remaining lemon zest, lots of chopped hazelnuts, and grated Parmesan cheese.

EXTRA TIP
If you are allergic to hazelnuts, don't like them, or simply don't have any on hand, try replacing them with almonds, pine nuts, or walnuts.

minutes

Crowd-pleaser

Family-friendly

One-pot macaroni and cheese

"Macaroni and cheese is perhaps the ultimate comfort food. I grew up thinking no version could ever top the bright orange, boxed version in terms of ease of preparation and taste – but I was very wrong. This one-pot take is just as easy, but tastes (and looks) so much better. I like using mezze ('half' in Italian) rigatoni here so the sauce can hide inside the tubes and ridges, but you can use any pasta shape you want. Use the highest quality aged white cheddar you can find and shred it yourself for the best outcome."

– Devan

6 servings

2 tbsp butter
2 tbsp flour
4 cups (950 ml) milk
3 cups (700 ml) water
1 lb (500 g) rigatoni
2 tsp salt
2 tsp mustard
2 tsp Worcestershire
   sauce
8 oz (225 g) shredded
   white cheddar
2 oz (60 g) grated
   Parmesan cheese
salt
pepper

1 Melt butter in a large pot over medium-high heat. Whisk in flour and let cook for approx. 1 min., whisking constantly. Once the roux (mixture of flour and butter) is light gold in color, whisk in about one-third of the milk and keep whisking until a thick, smooth sauce is formed. Whisk in the rest of the milk and add water. Bring to a simmer over medium heat, stirring occasionally.

2 Add rigatoni, salt, mustard, and Worcestershire sauce to the pot and mix. Let the pasta simmer for approx. 10 min., or until al dente. Stir occasionally.

3 Remove the pot from the heat and stir in the shredded white cheddar and grated Parmesan cheese. Keep stirring until the cheeses are melted and everything is very creamy. Season with salt and pepper to taste.

EXTRA TIP
You can add some sharp orange cheddar as well, or, if you're feeling fancy and want to switch it up a bit, use a mix of cheeses like Gruyère, fontina, or Emmentaler.

One-pot red pepper pasta with chicken

30 minutes

Crowd-pleaser

Family-friendly

"One-pot dishes are rightly regarded as secret weapons for quick and easy weeknight dinners – and not just because they save on dishes and after-dinner clean-up. For this recipe, the pasta cooks directly in the fragrant tomato-red pepper sauce so that it can truly absorb all the flavor. The pasta is quick to overcook, so be sure to pull it off the heat when it's al dente."

– Christian

6 servings

¾ lb (350 g) chicken breasts, boneless and skinless

3½ oz (100 g) bacon

2 red bell peppers

4 oz (100 g) cherry tomatoes

1 onion

1 clove garlic

2 tbsp olive oil

1 tsp dried oregano

1 tsp sugar

⅔ cup (150 ml) white wine

1¼ cups (300 ml) chicken stock

2 cups (500 ml) tomato purée

11 oz (300 g) penne

salt

pepper

basil for serving

grated Parmesan cheese for serving

1 Cut chicken into bite-size pieces and cube bacon. Core and slice bell peppers into thin strips. Halve cherry tomatoes. Peel and chop onion and mince garlic.

2 Heat olive oil in a large pot and sauté chicken for approx. 5 min. over medium heat. Add bacon, onion, and bell pepper and season with salt and pepper. Cook for approx. 3 min., then add garlic, dried oregano, sugar, and cherry tomatoes. Let cook until most of the liquid has evaporated, approx. 3 min.

3 Deglaze pot with white wine, chicken stock, and tomato purée, making sure to scrape the bottom of the pan for any brown bits. Bring everything to a boil, then add the penne. Cook until penne is al dente, approx. 10 min. Serve with basil and grated Parmesan cheese.

20
minutes

Crowd-
pleaser

Chinese cold noodles

"This is a basic recipe for Chinese-style cold noodles which can be amped up with shredded chicken, a hard-boiled egg, and soy or mung bean sprouts. You can substitute the wheat noodles with soba or rice noodles, if desired. The sauce can be made in a bigger batch to save for later, but I recommend making and using it fresh."

– Xueci

2 servings

½ cucumber
2 scallions
4 cloves garlic
4 tsp chili flakes
4 tsp sesame seeds
7 oz (200 g) dried Asian
  wheat noodles
⅓ cup (75 ml) vegetable oil
2 tbsp light soy sauce
1 tbsp rice vinegar
salt
sugar
toasted sesame oil
salted roasted peanuts for
  serving
cilantro for serving

1 Cut cucumber into matchsticks, or use a box grater to grate into long, thin pieces. Thinly slice scallions and peel and mince garlic.

2 Bring a pot of water to a boil and add noodles. Boil for approx. 1 min. less than the time stated on the package, then drain and rinse under cold running water. Toss with some toasted sesame oil so the noodles don't stick together.

3 Add scallions, garlic, chili flakes, and sesame seeds to a small bowl. Heat vegetable oil in a small frying pan over medium heat. Once it starts to shimmer, add to the bowl and mix to combine. Add soy sauce, rice vinegar, salt, and sugar to the sauce and mix again.

4 Divide noodles evenly between serving bowls and top with a few spoonfuls of sauce. Garnish with cucumber, peanuts, and cilantro. Mix thoroughly before enjoying.

EXTRA TIP
If you can't find any thin Chinese or Asian wheat noodles, you can use a long, thin Italian pasta like capellini or spaghettini.

1

2

3

4

Lemony pea and yogurt orzo

25
minutes

Vegetarian

From the
community

"This recipe was developed by our community member Gary Pollard. It sort of resembles a risotto thanks to the shape of the pasta (orzo is also called risoni due to its rice-like shape) and creamy yogurt sauce. By using frozen peas, you can make this spring-y dish all year round."

– Christian

2 servings

10½ oz (300 g) frozen
  peas
½ lemon
7 oz (200 g) orzo
2 cloves garlic
½ oz (15 g) parsley
½ cup (100 g) non-fat
  Greek yogurt
¼ cup (60 ml) olive oil
¼ cup (60 ml) milk
salt
pepper
mint for serving
grated Parmesan cheese
  for serving

1   Defrost peas. Zest lemon, then juice. Bring a pot of water to a boil and season generously with salt. Cook orzo according to the package instructions. Drain, rinse with cold water, and add back to the pot.

2   Drain defrosted peas and transfer just over half of them to a food processor with the peeled garlic cloves, parsley, Greek yogurt, olive oil, milk, lemon zest, and lemon juice. Season with salt and pepper, then blitz into a smooth sauce.

3   Add yogurt sauce and remaining peas to the pot with the orzo and mix to combine. Set the pot over low heat until everything is warmed through. Garnish with mint leaves, grated Parmesan cheese, and pepper.

EXTRA TIP
For a vegetarian
version, simply leave
out the Parmesan
cheese or replace
it with a sprinkle of
nutritional yeast.

50
minutes

Crowd-
pleaser

Summer

Swiss chard, Italian sausage, and white bean pasta

"Swiss chard is one of my favorite leafy greens and pairs really well with fatty, fennel-scented Italian sausage and creamy white beans. If you want to make this dish vegetarian, you can leave out the sausage completely, or, if you don't have Italian sausage on hand, you can use bacon or pancetta. Paccheri pasta might be hard to find, so use rigatoni or another tube-shaped pasta as a substitute."

– Devan

4 servings

14 oz (400 g) Swiss chard
10½ oz (300 g) Italian
  sausage
9 oz (250 g) canned white
  beans
2 shallots
2 sprigs rosemary
1 lb (500 g) paccheri pasta
½ cup (120 ml) white wine
2 tbsp butter
3½ oz (100 g) grated
  Parmesan cheese
salt
pepper
olive oil for frying
grated Parmesan cheese
  for serving

1 Trim Swiss chard and separate leaves from the stems. Slice stems and leaves into strips, then place in separate bowls. Remove Italian sausage meat from the casings. Drain beans and mash half of them with a fork. Peel and mince shallots.

2 Heat olive oil in a large frying pan over medium heat. Add rosemary sprigs and fry until fragrant. Remove from the pan and set aside. Add Italian sausage and fry until browned. Remove and set aside. Add Swiss chard stems and shallots to the frying pan and season with salt and pepper. Sauté over medium heat until soft and beginning to brown, approx. 5 min.

3 Meanwhile, bring a large pot of water to a boil, season generously with salt, and cook pasta according to the package instructions, reserving approx. 1 cup (240 ml) of pasta water before draining. Deglaze Swiss chard stems with white wine, then add butter, mashed white beans, and cooked Italian sausage. Stir to combine.

4 Pour some pasta water into the pan to form a sauce. Add remaining white beans and let simmer briefly to thicken. Add Swiss chard leaves and cook until tender, then add the pasta and grated Parmesan cheese and toss until well combined. Serve with fried rosemary and extra grated Parmesan cheese.

Scallion oil noodles

35
minutes

Vegan

"Nothing could be more minimalist or more satisfying than a bowl of scallion oil noodles (cong you mian). A Shanghai-style dish enjoyed all over China, the sauce magically turns scallions into an irresistible bowl of savory, aromatic goodness. If you don't have dark soy sauce, double the amount of light soy sauce and add a pinch more sugar, if desired."

– Xueci

2 servings

10 scallions
¼ cup (60 ml) light soy sauce
¼ cup (60 ml) dark soy sauce
2½ tbsp (30 g) sugar
⅔ cup (150 ml) vegetable oil
8 oz (200 g) dried Asian wheat noodles

1   Separate white and green parts of scallions and slice both into long pieces. In a bowl, mix light and dark soy sauces with sugar.

2   Heat vegetable oil in a frying pan over low heat. Add white scallions and fry on low for approx. 15 min. Add green parts of scallions and fry approx. 10 min. more. Add soy sauce mixture and simmer on low for approx. 2 min., then remove from heat.

3   Boil noodles according to the package instructions, then drain and divide among serving bowls. Spoon scallion oil over noodles and mix to combine. Reserve the rest of the oil in an airtight container in the fridge for up to 1 week.

60

minutes

Crowd-
pleaser

Make
ahead

Rigatoni with easy ragù

"Once you've made it a couple of times, you'll know this ragù by heart – it's that easy. Creating a soffritto (often used in Italian, Spanish, Portuguese, and Latin American cuisines) of onion, garlic, celery, and carrot gives the sauce a really aromatic base and, once you're done with all that chopping, it's a fairly hands-off recipe that yields delicious results. The addition of milk is a nifty Italian trick that helps to break down the meat and leads to an even richer result."

– Ruby

4 servings

1 onion
2 cloves garlic
2 carrots
2 stalks celery
¼ cup (60 ml) olive oil,
  divided
7 oz (200 g) ground beef
7 oz (200 g) ground pork
3 tbsp tomato paste
1 cup (240 ml) milk
½ cup (120 ml) red wine
1 cup (240 ml) beef stock
2 sprigs rosemary
1 bay leaf
14 oz (400 g) rigatoni
2 oz (60 g) grated
  Parmesan cheese
salt
pepper
grated Parmesan cheese
  for serving

1 Peel and roughly chop onion, garlic, and carrots. Roughly chop celery. Add to a food processor and use the pulse function until the pieces are very fine.

2 Heat half the olive oil in a large, heavy-bottomed pot over medium heat. Add ground beef and pork, season with salt and pepper, and sauté for approx. 5 min., or until well-browned. Remove the meat. Add remaining olive oil to the pot and sauté the onion, garlic, carrots, and celery for approx. 5 min., stirring often. Stir in tomato paste and cook until vegetables are soft and tomato paste begins to caramelize, approx. 5 min. more. Add meat back to the pot and stir to combine.

3 Add milk and bring everything to a simmer. Once milk is nearly evaporated, deglaze with red wine and simmer for another 5 min., then add beef stock, rosemary sprigs, and bay leaf. Let everything simmer over low heat for approx. 30 min.

4 Meanwhile, bring a large pot of water to a boil, season generously with salt, and cook rigatoni according to the package instructions, reserving approx. 1 cup (240 ml) of pasta water before draining. Before taking the ragù off the heat, remove bay leaf and rosemary sprigs, and stir in grated Parmesan cheese. Add rigatoni to the ragù, pouring in some pasta water to help combine everything if the mixture looks too dry. Season to taste and serve with extra Parmesan cheese.

EXTRA TIP
If you've got time on
your hands, you can keep
cooking the ragù on a low
heat until it reaches your
desired consistency. Store
leftovers in the fridge for
2–3 days, or freeze for up
to 2 months.

Meaty
Mains

Meatballs with horseradish mashed potatoes and gravy

60 minutes

Fall

Family-friendly

"I find meatballs a super comforting dish no matter what form or flavor they take, or how they're served up. Baked on a sheet pan, they can be a relatively hands-off weeknight dinner, but with just a bit more effort in the form of a braise, pan-fry, or glaze, they can also serve as something special when a spontaneous gathering of friends is heading over.

This recipe – developed by our chef Johanna – can play to just about any situation and is a winner for more than one reason. Served with mashed potatoes infused with the mustardy, sinus-clearing bite of horseradish, it's a classic combination served up in a new way. I'd recommend using this recipe as a base to apply all the new meatball-centric knowledge you'll learn in the pages to come."

– Devan

4 servings

FOR THE MEATBALLS

1 onion
1 clove garlic
1 bread roll
1 cup (240 ml) milk
14 oz (400 g) ground beef
1 egg
½ tsp ground allspice
1¾ oz (50 g) butter
1 tbsp flour
1 cup (240 ml) beef stock
1 cup (240 ml) heavy cream
salt
pepper
vegetable oil for frying
horseradish for serving

FOR THE HORSERADISH MASHED POTATOES

1 lb (500 g) potatoes
3½ oz (100 g) butter
½ cup (120 ml) milk
3½ tbsp (50 g) fresh
   horseradish
salt
nutmeg

EXTRA TIP
If you can't find fresh horseradish because it's not in season or isn't available, you can stir a bit of spicy brown mustard or jarred horseradish into the mashed potatoes instead.

1 Peel potatoes and add to a pot of cold water, then bring to a boil. Reduce heat and let potatoes simmer over medium heat for approx. 20 min., or until cooked through. While potatoes cook, dice peeled onion and mince peeled garlic for the meatballs. Crumble the bread roll into a bowl and pour milk over it.

2 Heat vegetable oil in a pan over medium heat, then add onion and garlic and sauté until translucent. In a large bowl, mix ground beef with sautéed onion, garlic, soaked and squeezed bread roll crumbs, and egg. Season with salt, pepper, and allspice. With your hands, form the mixture into meatballs.

3 Heat some vegetable oil in a cast-iron pan. Add meatballs and fry until browned on all sides and cooked through, approx. 15 min. Remove meatballs from heat, reserving meatball juices and browned bits in the pan.

4 Melt butter in the same pan and whisk in flour. Deglaze with beef stock and heavy cream. Bring to a boil and let the sauce simmer over medium until reduced.

5 Drain cooked potatoes and use a potato ricer to rice them into a bowl, or mash with a potato masher. Heat butter and milk in a small saucepan and season with salt and freshly grated nutmeg. Stir in the milk mixture and then grate horseradish into the mashed potatoes and mix to combine.

6 Add the meatballs to the gravy and let heat up for a few minutes. Serve meatballs and sauce together with mashed potatoes. Serve with more grated horseradish on top.

How to Make Magical Homemade Meatballs Without a Recipe

Meatballs are never not having a moment, so if you're not a believer already, it's about time you became one. They're loved all over the world, with variations rolled up on the regular in kitchens from China to Sweden, Germany to Japan.

Where to start

To make great meatballs without a recipe, you've got to get a handle on the importance of the 3 main components: the meat, the binders, and the additional flavorings. The emphasis you give to these components, and the ingredients you should reach for, depend on the meatball you're aiming to make, so ask yourself these questions before getting started: What flavor profile are you looking for – something classic, a veggie take, or maybe a spiced-up ball that can stand on its own? How do you plan to cook the meatballs – pan-fried for a crisper texture, boiled for something softer, or baked on a sheet pan for the sake of ease and a quick clean-up? How will they be served in the end – all sauced up, in a soup, or alongside a thick yogurt dip?

The meat

The base of any meatball is one, or multiple, ground meat(s). Beef, pork, veal, chicken, turkey, and lamb are the most common choices and can stand on their own, be combined with one another (think beef and pork for a classic Italian-American meatball or beef and lamb for a gamier take), or be stretched with other ingredients like cooked grains, lentils, or chopped mushrooms. Bacon or sausage are other meaty additions that offer some fat and additional flavor. It's even possible to create meatballs made solely out of sausage; just be careful not to add too many other additional flavorings and binders, as they don't need much.

If you'd prefer meatless, don't fear, there are plenty of options for you. To get that same heft and depth of flavor, a combination of cooked green or brown lentils and chopped mushrooms makes an excellent base, but you can also mix in oats, tempeh, tofu, quinoa, beans, chickpeas, or cauliflower.

The binders

The binder is very important when it comes to making your meatballs – it's what keeps them whole. You can use eggs, breadcrumbs, soaked bread, grated or creamy cheeses (think grated Parmesan, ricotta, or feta here), ground nuts, or a mixture of these ingredients to bind the balls and help them stay together while you cook them and as you eat them – no one wants a meatball that breaks apart all over the plate.

Depending on what your base is, what flavorings you want to add, and how you plan to cook your

meatballs, you might want to go easy or heavy on the binders. For example, if you plan to add plenty of additional flavorings and are going to pan-fry the meatballs, add a bit more of the binder(s) just to be on the safe side. However, a general rule of thumb when it comes to keeping your meatballs together is this: If you can scoop and roll your meatballs and they hold their shape on a plate, you should be fine. If you're still unsure, transfer them to the fridge for at least 15 minutes before cooking.

Additional flavorings

Now that the base and bindings for your balls are done, it's time to hop on the train to the only place on Earth where Guy Fieri could be king – Flavortown! When it comes to adding flavor to a meatball, there are rules of thumb, but few limitations. Classic choices include minced or grated onions, shallots, garlic, ginger, fresh herbs, minced vegetables like celery or carrot, tomato paste, dried or fresh spices, and sauces or other liquids like fish sauce or milk, plus salt and pepper, which – in my humble opinion – should season just about every meatball you make. To go out on a limb and experiment with things like minced lemongrass, preserved lemon, curry or harissa paste, or even minced dried fruits (think dates with lamb or apricots with pork) might sound crazy to the fundamentalist, but not to us.

6 Weeknight Meatball Variations to Try

There are at least 5 ways to cook a meatball: baking, braising, pan-frying, boiling, and steaming. Each has its benefits, but to really crisp up and brown the outside of your meatballs, bake or pan-fry them. Baking is my favorite method as it makes clean-up easy and is the most hands-off approach. If you're serving your meatballs in a sauce, braising the balls directly in the sauce might be your best option for building flavor and keeping the meatballs moist. Here are six variations of meatballs to get you started on your magical meatball journey.

Dill-y

1 8 oz (250 g) ground beef
2 8 oz (250 g) ground pork
3 2 tbsp crumbled feta cheese
4 1 egg
5 2 tbsp minced dill
6 ¼ cup (20 g) breadcrumbs

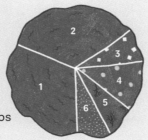

Mix all ingredients together, season with salt and pepper, and shape into balls. Pan-fry in some vegetable oil until golden-brown on all sides and cooked through. Serve with sour cream or yogurt, fresh dill or parsley, a spiced tomato sauce, and crusty, toasted hunks of bread.

Easy curry meatballs

1 1 lb (500 g) ground pork
2 2 tbsp minced cilantro
3 1 egg
4 ¼ cup (60 g) red curry paste

Mix all ingredients together, shape into balls, and chill in the fridge for 30 min. Boil in simmering water, then pan-fry or grill until golden-brown. Serve with steamed jasmine rice and fresh cilantro.

Italian-ish

1. 1 lb (500 g) ground turkey
2. ½ minced onion
3. 1 egg
4. ¼ cup (20 g) breadcrumbs
5. 1 tsp minced garlic
6. 2 tbsp minced parsley
7. ⅓ oz (10 g) grated Parmesan cheese
8. 1 tsp toasted fennel seeds
9. 1 oz (30 g) thawed, squeezed, and drained frozen spinach

Mix all ingredients together, season with salt and pepper, and shape into balls. Pan-fry in some olive oil, until brown on at least 2 sides. Add 12 oz (400 g) canned crushed tomatoes, a handful of fresh basil leaves, and 1 cup (240 ml) water to the pan. Cover and braise until meatballs are cooked through and sauce is reduced. Serve with cooked spaghetti, a drizzle of olive oil, and plenty of grated Parmesan cheese.

Spicy-sweet lemongrass

1. 1 lb (500 g) ground chicken
2. 1 tbsp minced lemongrass
3. 1 tsp minced ginger
4. 1 tsp minced garlic
5. ½ tsp chili flakes
6. 1 tbsp minced scallions
7. 2 tsp soy sauce
8. ⅓ cup (30 g) panko breadcrumbs

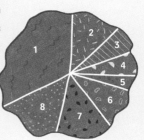

Add 5 tbsp honey, juice from ½ lemon, and 2 thinly sliced Thai chilis to a saucepan and bring to a boil. Let boil and reduce until thickened. Mix all ingredients together and shape into balls. Bake until cooked through, then brush with hot honey – broiling just for a few minutes until caramelized. Serve with steamed jasmine rice.

Ginger-y

1. 1 lb (500 g) ground pork
2. 1 tsp fish sauce
3. 1 tsp toasted sesame oil
4. 1 tbsp minced cilantro
5. 1 tsp minced garlic
6. ½ tsp sugar
7. 1 tsp minced ginger
8. ⅓ cup (30 g) panko breadcrumbs

Mix all ingredients together and shape into balls. Pan-fry in a little bit of vegetable oil until golden-brown on all sides and cooked through. Serve on top of a vegetable-studded glass or rice noodle salad.

Spiced lamb

1. 8 oz (250 g) ground lamb
2. 8 oz (250 g) ground beef
3. ½ minced onion
4. 1 tsp minced garlic
5. 2 tbsp minced parsley
6. 1 tbsp harissa paste
7. ½ tsp ground coriander
8. ½ tsp ground fennel seeds

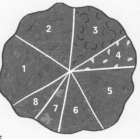

Mix all ingredients together, season with salt and pepper, and shape into balls. Bake or grill until cooked through. Serve with warm flatbread and a simple yogurt sauce spiked with garlic, lemon, and fresh herbs.

30 minutes

Low carb

Family-friendly

Easy baked chicken breasts with tomatoes and herbs

"This recipe is a great base for your weeknight dinner. Enjoy it as is, or serve the baked chicken breasts with a green salad or warm baguette. If you don't have a red onion on hand, swap in a white or yellow one, or even one or two shallots, instead."

– Johanna

4 servings

3 cloves garlic
1 onion
8 oz (250 g) cherry
    tomatoes
1 sprig thyme
4 sprigs parsley
1 sprig rosemary
2 oz (50 g) sun-dried
    tomatoes
4 chicken breasts,
    boneless and skinless
1 tsp dried oregano
3½ tbsp balsamic
    vinegar
½ cup (120 ml) olive oil
salt
pepper

1 Preheat the oven to 350 °F (180 °C). Peel and mince garlic. Peel and thinly slice onion. Halve cherry tomatoes. Remove thyme, parsley, and rosemary leaves from sprigs and chop together finely.

2 Add halved cherry tomatoes, sun-dried tomatoes, sliced onion, minced garlic, and half the chopped herbs to a baking dish. Pat chicken breasts dry with paper towels and place them in the baking dish.

3 Season chicken breasts with salt and pepper. Sprinkle with remaining chopped herbs and dried oregano. Add balsamic vinegar and olive oil to the dish and bake for approx. 20 min.

minutes

Low carb

Crowd-pleaser

Quick beef and mushroom ragù with creamy polenta

"The secret ingredient in this weeknight ragù is the shiitake mushrooms. They're very aromatic and go really well with beef. I used a top blade steak for this recipe, which is part of the cow's shoulder or chuck. It's best to remove it from the fridge approx. 30–60 min. before cooking so it can warm up to room temperature. Instead of polenta, you could serve the ragù with mashed potatoes or pasta."

– Christian

4 servings

FOR THE RAGÙ
1 onion
1 clove garlic
1 carrot
1 lb (500 g) top blade steak
1 tbsp flour
1 cup (240 ml) red wine
3 cups (750 ml) beef stock
¾ oz (20 g) dried shiitake
  mushrooms
1 bay leaf
4 juniper berries
salt
pepper
vegetable oil for frying

FOR THE POLENTA
2 sprigs thyme
5 cups (1.2 l) milk
7¼ oz (200 g) polenta
5½ oz (150 g) Parmesan
  cheese
salt
Parmesan cheese for
  serving

1 Peel and mince onion, garlic, and carrot.

2 Cut steak into bite-size chunks and season with salt. Heat vegetable oil in a large pot over medium heat and sear meat for approx. 5 min., or until well browned. Add onion, garlic, and carrot, and fry for approx. 5 min. more.

3 Sprinkle flour into the pot and let cook, stirring, for approx. 30 sec. Deglaze with red wine and let simmer until reduced by about half. Add beef stock, dried shiitake mushrooms, bay leaf, and juniper berries and let the ragù simmer for approx. 45 min.

4 In the meantime, pick thyme leaves from the stem and finely chop them. Add milk to a pot and bring to a boil. Whisk in polenta, then add thyme leaves and a pinch of salt. Let the polenta simmer for approx. 15 min. over medium-low heat, stirring regularly. Just before serving, remove the pot from the heat, grate Parmesan cheese into it, and stir to combine. Serve ragù with polenta and more Parmesan cheese, if desired.

EXTRA TIP
If you have more time,
let the ragù simmer
for longer so that
the flavors can really
develop.

60
minutes

Low carb

Crowd-
pleaser

Chicken cacciatore

"In Italy, 'pollo alla cacciatora' or 'hunter-style chicken' has many regional variations. Outside of Italy however, the most well-known version is similar to this one, but the recipe offers plenty of options for adjustments. For example, you could use white instead of red wine or swap out the button mushrooms for porcini – depending on the season. You can also add some capers or use another type of olive. I like to serve this dish with toasted bread, but polenta, pasta, or even rice also work well."

– Christian

4 servings

1 onion
4 cloves garlic
1 red bell pepper
1 green bell pepper
7¼ oz (200 g) button
  mushrooms
2 stalks celery
2 sprigs thyme
2 sprigs rosemary
3 leaves sage
2 tbsp olive oil
4 chicken breasts,
  boneless and skinless
2 bay leaves
2 tbsp tomato paste
5¼ oz (150 g) Kalamata
  olives
1 cup (240 ml) red wine
10 oz (300 g) canned
  crushed tomatoes
⅔ cup (150 ml) water *or broth*
salt
pepper
toasted bread for serving

1 Preheat the oven to 350 °F (180 °C). Peel and mince onion and garlic. Thinly slice bell pepper, mushrooms, and celery. Remove thyme and rosemary leaves from stems, add sage, and finely chop herbs together.

2 Heat olive oil in an ovenproof pan over medium-high heat. Add chicken breasts, season with salt and pepper, and sear for approx. 3 min. on each side. Remove chicken from the pan and set aside.

3 Add onion, garlic, bell pepper, mushrooms, and celery to the pan and sauté for approx. 3 min. Add bay leaves and tomato paste and stir to combine. Add olives, then deglaze the pan with red wine. Add canned tomatoes, water, and chopped herbs.

4 Nestle chicken back into the pan and cover with the sauce. Season with salt and pepper. Transfer the pan to the oven and bake for approx. 30 min. Serve with toasted bread.

3.25 Simon
Good not great
lacks flavour
drizzle balsamic
vinegar @ end

Roasted pork chops with caramelized pears and thyme

45 minutes

Low carb

Family-friendly

"For this recipe, it's important to use very thick-cut pork chops on the bone, which you can ask for directly at the butcher's counter of most grocery stores. Make sure to fry the meat on all sides for the best flavor and sear. I like to serve these with potatoes or gnocchi to make it a more satisfying meal, but it's also great as is."

– Christian

2 servings

2 pears
3 shallots
2 pork chops, thick-cut and bone-in
1 tbsp butter
1 tbsp olive oil
8 sprigs thyme
¼ cup (50 ml) orange liqueur
salt
pepper
olive oil for frying

1 Preheat the oven to 350°F (180°C). Quarter and core pears lengthwise, then slice the quarters in half again. Peel and halve shallots. Heat a grill pan over medium-high heat and add some oil. Season both sides of pork chops with salt and grill in the hot pan on each side until brown grill marks appear or there is a nice sear, approx. 10 min. in total. Remove and set aside.

2 Heat butter and olive oil in the same pan and add sliced pears, shallots, and thyme sprigs. Sauté for approx. 5 min. and season with salt and pepper. Add orange liqueur and let simmer for approx. 30 sec. more.

3 Transfer pear mixture to a baking dish and place pork chops on top. Bake for approx. 20 min. Let pork chops rest for approx. 5 min. before serving.

EXTRA TIP
If you don't have or don't want to use orange liqueur, replace it with a 1:1 mixture of orange juice and water.

45

minutes

★

Crowd-
pleaser

Shrimp and sausage gumbo

"Gumbo is a spicy soup-slash-stew from Louisiana that showcases the mixed culinary history from the region with influences from Africa, Spain, and France, among others. It's typically prepared with seafood, poultry, smoked sausage, and the 'Holy Trinity' of vegetables: celery, green bell peppers, and onions. This is a simpler take, featuring just shrimp and sausage, but you could add chicken or duck if you'd like."

– Johanna

4 servings

12⅓ oz (350 g) smoked
  sausage
1 green bell pepper
3 stalks celery
1 onion
3 cloves garlic
1 Thai chili
4 scallions
3 tbsp olive oil
2 oz (50 g) butter
2 oz (50 g) flour
2 bay leaves
9 oz (260 g) canned
  crushed tomatoes
1⅔ cups (400 ml)
  chicken stock
1 tsp paprika
½ tsp dried thyme
8 oz (225 g) shrimp,
  peeled and deveined
salt
pepper
rice for serving

1 Chop sausage into bite-size pieces. Dice bell pepper and celery. Chop peeled onion and garlic, and the chili. Thinly slice scallions and set aside.

2 Add olive oil, butter, and flour to a large pot over medium heat and stir for approx. 6–10 min., or until the roux (mixture of flour, butter, and oil) has turned light brown. Add onions, garlic, chili, bell peppers, and celery to the pot, and sauté for approx. 5 min.

3 Add smoked sausage, bay leaves, canned crushed tomatoes, chicken stock, paprika, and dried thyme to the pot. Season with salt and pepper and bring to a boil. Once boiling, cover and let simmer for approx. 15 min. Add shrimp to pot and cook for another 5 min. Serve gumbo with rice and sprinkle with sliced scallions.

1

2

3

45
minutes

Fall

Schnitzel with mushroom gravy

"In order for the schnitzel to cook evenly, it should almost float in a pool of clarified butter. If you can't find or don't want to use the traditional veal cutlets, you can also use pork cutlets. Panko is not a classic choice for the breading, but I find it fries up even crisper than regular breadcrumbs and is a definite upgrade. If you don't have any around, regular breadcrumbs work just the same. For an even more satisfying dinner, serve with spätzle, french fries, or fried or boiled potatoes."

– Christian

4 servings

1 onion
1 clove garlic
1 lb (500 g) button
  mushrooms
2 tbsp vegetable oil
2 tbsp butter
4½ oz (125 g) flour
¼ cup (50 ml) chicken
  stock
1 cup (240 ml) heavy cream
4 veal cutlets
1 egg
3½ oz (100 g) panko
  breadcrumbs
3 oz (80 g) clarified butter
salt
pepper
parsley for serving
lemon for serving

1 Peel and mince onion and garlic. Clean and halve button mushrooms. Heat vegetable oil in a frying pan over medium heat and fry mushrooms for approx. 10 min., or until browned. Add butter, onions, and garlic and keep frying until the onions are translucent.

2 Add 1 tbsp of the flour and sauté for approx. 1 min. Deglaze with chicken stock and heavy cream, and season with salt and pepper to taste. Let the mushroom gravy simmer over low heat while you move on to cook the schnitzel.

3 Season the veal cutlets with salt and pepper on both sides. Whisk egg in a shallow plate or bowl. Add remaining flour and breadcrumbs to separate shallow plates or bowls. Dredge each cutlet first in flour, then in beaten egg, and finally coat with breadcrumbs on both sides.

4 Add clarified butter to a frying pan over medium heat and fry each cutlet on both sides for approx. 3 min., or until golden-brown and cooked through. Serve schnitzel with mushroom gravy, chopped parsley, and lemon wedges.

35
minutes

Low carb

Crowd-
pleaser

Grilled chicken piccata

"Chicken piccata is a beloved, classic dish in the United States – where I grew up – and for good reason: Recipes don't come more weeknight-friendly than this. The ingredient list is plucked straight from a well-stocked pantry, and the lemon-butter sauce spiked with briny capers is one every home cook should know how to make – you'll enjoy it just as much with veal (as in the original Italian tradition), fish, or even just sauteéd vegetables. Be sure to serve it with a side of pasta or crusty garlic bread to soak up every drop."

– Julie

4 servings

4 chicken breasts,
  boneless and skinless
1 shallot
1 clove garlic
2 lemons
½ oz (15 g) parsley
½ cup (120 ml) white wine
¾ cup (185 ml) chicken
  stock
1 tbsp flour
2 oz (50 g) capers
1 oz (30 g) butter
salt
pepper
olive oil for frying

1 Carefully slice each chicken breast in half horizontally to make thin cutlets. Peel and mince shallot and garlic. Thinly slice one lemon and juice the other. Finely chop parsley.

2 Heat a grill pan over medium-high heat and brush with olive oil. When hot, grill chicken, flipping once, until cooked through, approx. 5 min. per side.

3 In a second frying pan, heat olive oil over medium heat. Add chopped garlic and shallot and cook until fragrant, approx. 2–3 min. Turn heat up to medium-high and add white wine. Simmer for approx. 1 min., then add chicken stock. Whisk flour into the pan until smooth and continue to cook for approx. 4–5 min., until thickened.

4 Add lemon juice, capers, and butter, and mix until butter is melted. Season with salt and pepper to taste. Add chicken breasts to the pan with the caper sauce and spoon more sauce over the top. Top with lemon slices and sprinkle with parsley.

EXTRA TIP
A grill or grill pan is not essential for this recipe, though it's a fun twist on the classic. If you're not using one, swap in a frying pan and make it a one-pan meal to boot.

Beef and broccoli stir-fry

30 minutes

Low carb

Family-friendly

"This stir-fry is a quick weeknight dinner relying on the classic combination of beef and broccoli tossed in a glossy, savory, and simple stir-fry sauce bursting with ginger, garlic, and just a hint of heat. You can enjoy this dish as is or serve it with rice."

– Christian

4 servings

FOR THE BEEF AND BROCCOLI

1 lb (500 g) sirloin steak
3 tbsp soy sauce
½ lime
2 cloves garlic
⅓ oz (10 g) ginger
1 Thai chili
3 scallions
14 oz (400 g) broccoli
vegetable oil for frying

FOR THE SAUCE

1 cup (240 ml) beef stock
2 tbsp cane sugar
3 tbsp soy sauce
1½ tbsp cornstarch
½ lime

1 Slice sirloin into thin strips. Add half the soy sauce and juice from half a lime to a bowl. Add beef, tossing to coat, and set aside to marinate.

2 In a liquid measuring cup, whisk together the beef stock, cane sugar, soy sauce, cornstarch, and lime juice. Set aside. Peel and mince garlic and ginger. Thinly slice chili and scallions. Cut broccoli into small florets.

3 Heat vegetable oil in a frying pan over medium heat. Sauté the beef for approx. 2–3 min. Remove the meat from the pan and set aside. Heat some more oil in the frying pan and add garlic, ginger, scallions, and chili. Sauté for approx. 3 min. Add broccoli florets and sauté for approx. 5 min. longer. Return the meat to the pan and add the sauce. Mix well and cook until the sauce is thickened, approx. 5 min.

40
minutes

Low carb

Family-
friendly

Crispy garlicky chicken

"A super easy chicken recipe that, once you've made it a few times, is easily doable without even referencing the recipe. Don't be scared off by all the garlic – it becomes a bit milder and sweeter when roasted, so the end result isn't overpoweringly garlicky."

– Devan

4 servings

6 cloves garlic
3 scallions
4 chicken legs
1 tbsp olive oil
3 tbsp butter
4 tbsp rice vinegar
salt
pepper
jasmine rice for serving

1 Preheat the oven to 425°F (220°C). Peel and crush garlic cloves and place in a bowl. Thinly slice scallions, adding the white parts to the bowl with the garlic and setting the green parts aside for garnish.

2 Separate chicken legs into thighs and drumsticks. Brush both sides of the chicken with olive oil and season with salt and pepper.

3 Place an ovenproof pot over medium heat. Add the chicken thighs, skin-side down, and let cook for approx. 5 min. Turn up the heat to high and cook for approx. 10 min. more. Flip the chicken and let cook for approx. 5 min. Turn off the heat and scatter the crushed garlic cloves and white ends of the scallions into the pot. Transfer the pot to the oven and roast the chicken for approx. 15 min.

4 Remove from the oven, then remove chicken from the pot and set aside to rest. Scoop out the garlic cloves and transfer to a food processor or mortar and pestle. Season with salt and blend or mash into a paste. Place the pot over medium heat and add butter, stirring to melt. Deglaze with rice wine vinegar, scraping the bottom of the pan. Let cook for approx. 2 min., then stir the garlic paste back into the pan sauce. For serving, drizzle chicken with the pan sauce, sprinkle with scallion greens, and serve with jasmine rice.

5-ingredient Italian sausage ragù with polenta

25

minutes

Crowd-pleaser

Family-friendly

"Ragù is not usually considered when it comes to quick weeknight dinners, but this recipe (and the others like it) has a few tricks up its sleeve, relying on pre-seasoned, quick-cooking Italian sausage and a simple aromatic base. For the best depth of flavor and overall taste, use a high-quality Italian sausage and serve the ragù with grated Pecorino or Parmesan cheese."

– Devan

2 servings

FOR THE RAGÙ
1 onion
2 sprigs thyme
8 oz (225 g) Italian sausage
14 oz (400 g) canned crushed tomatoes
salt
pepper
olive oil for frying
thyme for serving

FOR THE POLENTA
3 cups (800 ml) water
4¼ oz (120 g) polenta
2 tbsp butter
salt

EXTRA TIP
No polenta? You can serve the ragù with pasta instead. This dish is also easily scaled up or down.

1 Peel and thinly slice onion. Remove thyme leaves from sprigs and chop. Heat some olive oil in a large frying pan over medium heat. Remove Italian sausage from the casings, add to the frying pan, and break up with a cooking spoon as it browns. Season with salt and pepper, and fry for approx. 8 min., or until the sausage is well browned and crispy, then remove from the frying pan with a slotted spoon.

2 Drain half the fat from the frying pan, add sliced onion, and sauté for approx. 5 min. or until translucent. Add chopped thyme, canned crushed tomatoes, and Italian sausage back to the pan. Reduce heat and let the ragù simmer while you make the polenta.

3 Add water to a pot and bring to a simmer. Pour in polenta, reduce heat, and keep whisking constantly for a smooth texture, approx. 5 min. Turn heat to low and cook for approx. 10 min. more, or until thickened and cooked through. Remove from heat, add butter, and season with salt. Serve polenta with sausage ragù on top, and garnish with fresh thyme if desired.

55
minutes

Low carb

Make
ahead

Miso pork stuffed eggplant

*"Miso is a great and really versatile Japanese condiment
made from fermented soy beans. One really delicious way
to use it is to make 'nikumiso,' a ground meat 'sauce' made
with pork braised in miso and typically served with rice or
noodles, or in sandwiches or salads. This recipe stuffs it into
cute roasted eggplant cups."*

– Xueci

4 servings

4 eggplants
¾ oz (20 g) ginger
2 scallions
3 tbsp sugar
4 tbsp red miso paste
1 tbsp soy sauce
⅓ cup (80 ml) sake
14 oz (400 g) ground pork
vegetable oil
sesame seeds for serving

1 Preheat the oven to 350°F (180°C). Peel eggplants lengthwise, leaving space between peels to create a striped pattern. Cut off both ends, then halve widthwise. Mince ginger and thinly slice scallions.

2 Use a spoon to carve out the center of the eggplants, leaving ¾ in.–1 in. (2–3 cm) on the sides and bottom. Chop the eggplant flesh that was removed from the center of the eggplants and set aside. Transfer eggplant cups to a baking dish, brush with oil, and bake for approx. 20 min.

3 In the meantime, whisk sugar, miso paste, soy sauce, and sake together. Heat vegetable oil in a frying pan and fry ginger until fragrant. Add ground pork and fry until browned. Add chopped eggplant and fry. Add miso sauce, stirring to combine. Stir-fry until the pork is glossy and covered with sauce. It will appear a bit dry. If there is a lot of liquid left in the pan, let it keep cooking until most of it evaporates.

4 Remove eggplants from the oven. Carefully stuff the pork mixture into the baked eggplants, and return to the oven. Reduce the temperature to 325°F (165°C), and bake for approx. 10 min. more. Garnish with scallions and sesame seeds before serving.

EXTRA TIP
If you want to make a vegetarian version, use shiitake mushrooms, firm tofu, or tempeh instead of ground pork.

Chicken with creamy sun-dried tomato sauce

35
minutes

Family-
friendly

From the
community

"This recipe by our community member Irina Panarina is one of our most popular community recipes for a reason. It's quick, easy to prepare, and made with lots of simple ingredients. Serve it with a fresh baguette, rice, or pasta."

– Johanna

2 servings

3½ oz (100 g) sun-dried
   tomatoes
2 cloves garlic
2 chicken breasts, boneless
   and skinless
2 oz (50 g) Parmesan cheese
2 tbsp butter, divided
½ tsp chili flakes
1 cup (240 ml) chicken stock
½ tsp dried thyme
½ tsp dried oregano
½ tsp dried basil
½ cup (120 ml) heavy cream
salt
pepper
flour
basil for serving
baguette for serving

EXTRA TIP
If you don't have sun-dried tomatoes, you can simply swap in cherry tomatoes.

1 Halve sun-dried tomatoes and set aside. Peel and mince garlic and set aside. Cut chicken breasts into bite-size pieces. Sprinkle with flour and season with salt and pepper, then toss to coat the chicken in the flour. Grate Parmesan cheese.

2 Preheat the oven to 350 °F (180 °C). Melt half the butter in an ovenproof pan over medium-high heat. Once melted and sizzling, add chicken and sear for approx. 3 min., or until golden-brown on both sides. Melt remaining butter in the frying pan with the chicken. Add minced garlic and chili flakes, and cook for approx. 2 min., stirring frequently, until fragrant.

3 Add chicken stock, sun-dried tomatoes, grated Parmesan cheese, thyme, oregano, basil, and heavy cream to the pan and stir to combine. Bring to a boil, then reduce heat and simmer for approx. 3–5 min., or until slightly thickened. Transfer the frying pan into the oven and bake chicken for approx. 15 min., or until cooked through. Garnish with fresh basil and serve with a sliced baguette.

60
minutes

Family-
friendly

Beef tenderloin with green beans, mashed potatoes, and mustard sauce

"This recipe makes it possible for you to enjoy a take on the classic meat-and-potatoes Sunday dinner, even on a weeknight. Making the mustard sauce in the same frying pan as the steak allows you to incorporate all those browned-up bits and flavors into the sauce to make it extra savory. The key to incredibly creamy mashed potatoes? Mash them while they're still warm, then incorporate warm cream and butter."

– Christian

2 servings

FOR THE MASHED POTATOES
14 oz (400 g) potatoes
⅔ cup (150 ml) heavy
  cream
1¾ oz (50 g) butter
salt
nutmeg

FOR THE GREEN BEANS
7 oz (200 g) green beans
2 sprigs summer savory
4 strips bacon
salt
pepper

**FOR THE BEEF TENDERLOIN
AND MUSTARD SAUCE**
1 lb (500 g) beef tenderloin
1 shallot
¼ cup (50 ml) white wine
¼ cup (50 ml) apple juice
1 cup (240 ml) heavy cream
1 tsp mustard
2 tsp grainy mustard
1½ oz (40 g) butter
salt
pepper
vegetable oil for frying

1 For the mashed potatoes, peel and dice potatoes. Add them to a pot with cold water. Add salt, bring to a boil, then reduce heat to medium. Cook for approx. 15–20 min., or until very tender. In the meantime, add heavy cream and butter to a pot over medium heat and let warm through until the butter is melted, then reduce heat to low. Once the potatoes are done, drain and use a potato ricer to rice them directly back into the pot. Add cream-butter mixture to the potatoes and mix to combine. Season with salt and freshly grated nutmeg to taste and keep warm.

2 Trim green beans and blanch them in a pot of boiling water, then drain and add them to a bowl of cold water. Finely chop summer savory and bacon. Fry bacon in a frying pan until crispy. Add blanched green beans and chopped summer savory. Season with salt and pepper and fry for approx. 1–2 min.

3 Cut beef tenderloin into two servings and season with salt and pepper. Peel and mince shallot. Heat vegetable oil in a frying pan over medium-high heat, add steaks, and fry for approx. 3 min. on each side. Remove from the pan.

4 In the same pan, fry shallot until translucent. Deglaze with white wine and apple juice. Add heavy cream, mustard, grainy mustard, and butter. Stir to combine and let simmer until the sauce is thickened and creamy. Season with salt and pepper to taste. Transfer steaks back to the pan and cook for approx. 3 min. over medium-low heat. Serve with mashed potatoes and green beans.

Out of
the Oven

Simple sheet pan salmon

45
minutes

Low carb

Family-
friendly

"Sheet pan dinners are all-in-one meals that come together on a single baking sheet and offer simple, hands-off prep, and fewer dishes to do after the meal. Most of these types of recipes offer plenty of vegetables, in addition to proteins such as seafood, meat, or tofu, but to do them right, you have to know how to use time and temperature to your advantage – which we'll show you how to do in the pages that follow.

For this recipe, I kept the salmon fillet whole so it doesn't get dry in the oven but stays wonderfully juicy, tender, and pink inside."

– Christian

4 servings

1¾ lb (800 g) rainbow
  potatoes
4 tbsp olive oil, divided
1⅓ lb (600 g) green
  asparagus
1 clove garlic
4 tbsp honey
2 lemons, divided
½ tsp fennel seeds,
  crushed
1½ lb (700 g) salmon fillet
salt
pepper
sugar
flaky sea salt for serving

1 Preheat the oven to 350 °F (180 °C). Halve potatoes and transfer them to a baking sheet. Drizzle with half the olive oil and season with salt. Bake for approx. 15 min.

2 In the meantime, trim off the ends of the asparagus and add the stalks to a bowl with the remaining olive oil, salt, and sugar. Stir to combine and let marinate. Once the roasting time for the potatoes is over, push them to either side of the baking sheet and add asparagus to the center. Bake for approx. 15 min.

3 While asparagus is baking, peel and mince garlic. Add to a small bowl with honey, the juice of one lemon, and crushed fennel seeds. Season with salt and pepper, then stir to combine. Remove the baking sheet from the oven and carefully add the salmon fillet on top of the asparagus in the center of the baking sheet. Brush with the garlic-honey mixture.

4 Turn on the broil function of the oven. Halve and thinly slice the remaining lemon and place the lemon slices on top of the salmon. Return the baking sheet to the oven and broil until the lemon slices are caramelized and the salmon is just cooked through. Sprinkle with flaky sea salt before serving.

EXTRA TIP
The colorful potatoes are a real eye-catcher on both the baking sheet and your plate, but you can use regular new potatoes as well.

The Perfect Sheet Pan Dinner

Sheet pan dinners are back-pocket "recipes" for success. We'll guide you through the right temperatures and oven settings to use, and show you how to pack as much variety as possible onto your baking sheet so you can be set up for a winning weeknight meal with just a few ingredients.

While many recipes for sheet pan dinners are destined to fail from the start, with the tips and tricks you'll learn here, you'll never have to worry about dealing with ingredients both overcooked and undercooked, or that lack texture, color, or flavor. From the different ingredients best suited to a sheet pan meal, to the ways you can add flavor with marinades and glazes, here's what you need to know to create tasty, foolproof sheet pan dinners.

Before you get started

Generally speaking, the thicker and firmer the raw ingredient, the longer it needs in the oven. Sweet potatoes, pumpkin, and beets need more time to cook than, say, bell peppers, chickpeas, or asparagus. If you want to make things easier and achieve more even cooking, adjust the size of the pieces according to the ingredient's cooking time. This means cutting vegetables that need longer to cook into smaller pieces than vegetables with a shorter cooking time. Depending on the ingredient and your desired texture and color, you should be roasting ingredients anywhere between 350 °F (180 °C) and 400 °F (200 °C) – lower and longer for a softer texture, higher and shorter to retain a bit of bite and get plenty of roasty, toasty color.

THE FOUNDATIONS OF A SHEET PAN MEAL

Something hearty and satisfying should make up the foundation of a meal like this, so think potatoes, sweet potatoes, beets, parsnips, carrots, or parsley roots as veg-forward bases, or opt for a whole pork tenderloin for something meatier (more on that later).

THE VEGETABLES Wondering which ingredients are sheet-pan-dinner-friendly and which are better left out? Avoid mushrooms and tender vegetables like spinach, which tend to soften, release a lot of liquid, or shrivel up easily. An exception here should definitely be made for shiitake mushrooms, which work really well here and help add that fifth taste, or umami, to a sheet pan dinner.

Great vegetables for roasting include broccoli, cauliflower, fennel, asparagus, bok choy, peppers, Brussels sprouts, zucchini, onions, and tomatoes, which can be combined and mixed as you like – just don't forget a marinade or some sort of glaze or rub, which will help add variety to your regular sheet-pan-dinner routine. Also, perhaps surprisingly, salad varieties with a firm stem, such as romaine lettuce, endive, or radicchio, taste quite good after a short stint in the oven or on the grill, so think about adding these for some variety as well.

THE PROTEIN Chicken thighs, pork tenderloin, cod, tofu, seitan, tempeh – there are many protein choices that take well to roasting. The latter options have the advantage of not needing to reach a certain internal temperature, but all of them benefit from a toss or brushing down with a simple marinade before roasting.

DIFFERENT MARINADES Beyond the classic "marinade" of olive oil, salt, and pepper, sheet pan dinners are a nice opportunity to try experimenting with ingredients and flavors. Brush tofu or vegetables with miso, sesame oil, or curry paste, or add brown sugar to a marinade to give them a hint of sweetness and help aid caramelization. Toss crushed whole seeds (think fennel, coriander, or cumin) into the mix or sprinkle in a pinch of cayenne for heat. If you've got time on your hands, let your ingredients marinate for a couple of hours before roasting.

DIPS AND TOPPINGS A well-rounded meal usually benefits from a mix of different textures, and a creamy dip or crispy topping will help round out most sheet pan dinners. Dips like a thick garlicky yogurt, an herby pesto, or even creamy hummus play well with a lot of different vegetables and proteins. For added crunch, top with something like crispy fried onions, chopped walnuts, or sunflower seeds.

What about leftovers?

A sheet pan full of vegetables and proteins is great for a quick dinner, but can also be called upon for handy, hands-off meal prep and give you a great foundation to pull from throughout the week. Feel like a salad? Match roasted root vegetables like beets, carrots, and parsnips with fresh baby spinach and a simple vinaigrette. If you have simple pumpkin or sweet potatoes leftover from your sheet pan dinner, try blending them into a creamy sauce for pasta. Whether you want to eat them cold from the fridge or turn them into something else completely, sheet pan leftovers are worth setting yourself up for.

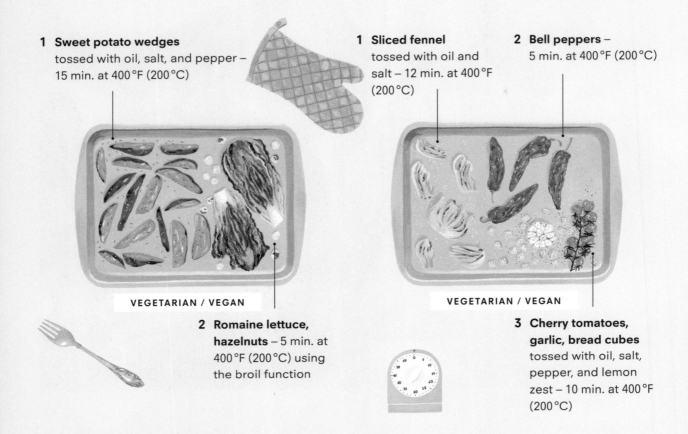

1 Sweet potato wedges
tossed with oil, salt, and pepper –
15 min. at 400 °F (200 °C)

1 Sliced fennel
tossed with oil and
salt – 12 min. at 400 °F
(200 °C)

2 Bell peppers –
5 min. at 400 °F (200 °C)

VEGETARIAN / VEGAN

**2 Romaine lettuce,
hazelnuts** – 5 min. at
400 °F (200 °C) using
the broil function

VEGETARIAN / VEGAN

**3 Cherry tomatoes,
garlic, bread cubes**
tossed with oil, salt,
pepper, and lemon
zest – 10 min. at 400 °F
(200 °C)

Simple Sheet Pan Recipes for Every Day

These "recipes" are a complete dinner on one sheet pan, taking the simple theories from the previous pages and putting them into practice. The 6 ideas outlined here are quick to put together and can be eaten tonight or prepared ahead. Plus, they're totally open for modification according to your own tastes, the seasons, or even what you have in the fridge.

Each of these illustrations should be seen as a recipe. Ingredients listed behind the number 1 need the longest time in the oven, and ingredients listed after 2 and 3 are to be added afterward, based on the instructions. What's still missing? Dips, fresh herbs, and more, which you can mix and match based on our tips on the previous pages to suit your tastes.

1 Cauliflower florets tossed with coconut oil, curry paste, salt, sugar, and lime – 15 min. at 400 °F (200 °C)

2 Chickpeas, garlic, ginger tossed with coconut oil, salt, and ground coriander – 10 min. at 350 °F (180 °C)

1 Pork tenderloin wrapped with bacon, tossed with salt and pepper – 10 min. at 350 °F (180 °C)

VEGETARIAN / VEGAN

3 Chopped peanuts – 5 min. at 350 °F (180 °C)

MEAT

2 Carrots, shallots tossed with oil, salt, pepper, and sugar – 15 min. at 350 °F (180 °C)

1 Chicken thighs tossed with maple syrup and salt – 20 min. at 325 °F (160 °C)

2 Blanched green beans, red onions tossed with oil, salt, and pepper – 10 min. at 350 °F (180 °C)

1 Cod tossed with sake, miso, and sugar, **bok choy, shiitake mushrooms** tossed with sesame oil, salt, and lime juice – 10 min. at 425 °F (220 °C)

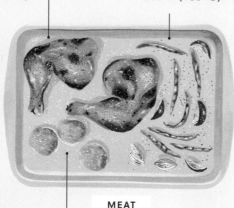

MEAT

3 Puff pastry brushed with an egg wash – 12 min. at 425 °F (220 °C)

FISH

2 3 min. using the broil function

5-ingredient oven-roasted chicken thighs and red peppers

"If there's some liquid left in the pan after you've baked the chicken thighs, carefully drain it and stir in some diced butter for a deliciously creamy and fatty-flavored spread to schmear all over your baguette."

– Devan

2 servings

2 red bell peppers
2 shallots
1 lemon
4 chicken thighs
2 sprigs rosemary
salt
pepper
olive oil for frying
baguette for serving

1 Preheat the oven to 425°F (220°C). Core and slice bell peppers into thick strips. Peel and thinly slice shallots and quarter lemon. Pat chicken thighs dry on both sides with a paper towel.

2 Heat a cast-iron pan over medium-high heat. Add some olive oil to the pan, then add bell peppers, shallots, and rosemary sprigs and sauté for approx. 4 min. Season with salt and pepper. Add half the lemon quarters to the pan and place the chicken thighs on top, skin-side up. Brush chicken with some olive oil and season with salt and pepper.

3 Transfer pan to the preheated oven and roast until chicken is cooked through, approx. 20 min. Turn the broil function of your oven to high and cook for another 5–10 min., or until chicken skin is golden-brown and crisp. Let rest for at least 10 min. before serving with the remaining lemon wedges and a warm baguette.

EXTRA TIP
This oven-roasted chicken also works well served with rice instead of crusty bread. Check out the best way to prepare on page 42.

60 minutes

Vegetarian

Make ahead

Simple onion tart

"I always like to have a few versatile recipes in my back pocket that can be adjusted as needed for a different look or flavor. Onion quiche is one example, and here I turned it into an onion tart by swapping shortcrust with phyllo dough for the base. Instead of using yellow onions, I used red for a colorful contrast and slightly different flavor. To see the beautiful purple-red filling, leave plenty of room in the center and fold the phyllo over itself around the edges of the filling."

– Lisa

8 servings

2¼ lb (1 kg) red onions
2 tbsp butter
4 tbsp olive oil
¼ cup (50 ml) white wine
2 tbsp white wine vinegar
2 tsp dried thyme
2 tbsp cane sugar
3½ oz (100 g) walnuts
5 sheets phyllo dough
5¼ oz (150 g) crème
  fraîche
salt
pepper
nutmeg
olive oil for brushing

1 Peel and very thinly slice red onions. Heat butter and olive oil in a frying pan over medium heat, until butter is melted. Add onions and fry for approx. 10 min., or until soft and translucent. Season with salt, then add white wine, white wine vinegar, and dried thyme. Keep frying until nearly all the liquid has evaporated and the onions are relatively dry. Add cane sugar, mix to combine, then set aside to cool.

2 Preheat the oven to 350 °F (180 °C). Transfer walnuts to a baking sheet and roast in the oven until golden-brown, approx. 8 min. Lay a sheet of phyllo dough out, brush with olive oil, and lay into a tart pan. Repeat with all sheets of phyllo. They should overlap to create a sturdy crust and there should be plenty of overhang. Add toasted walnuts into the bottom of the tart.

3 Mix cooled onions with crème fraîche and season with salt, pepper, and freshly grated nutmeg to taste. Spread the onion mixture over the walnuts and smooth it out.

4 Fold the overhang of the phyllo dough towards the center to cover just the sides of the filling. Brush the top of the phyllo with more olive oil. Bake the tart for approx. 20–25 min., or until the crust is golden-brown.

40

minutes

Crowd-
pleaser

Salmon, broccoli, and potato casserole with capers and mozzarella

"As in life, the success of a recipe is all in the details. For this casserole, 'the details' take the form of salty capers, vibrant white wine vinegar and lemon, and spicy Thai chili. Together, these ingredients turn an otherwise simple casserole into a delightfully surprising dinner experience. If you have fresh tarragon or basil, tear some on top before serving."

– Christian

2 servings

14 oz (400 g) new potatoes
1 head broccoli
1 Thai chili
1 clove garlic
2 tbsp capers
2 tbsp white wine vinegar
2 tbsp olive oil
1 tbsp lemon juice
1 lb (500 g) salmon fillet
10½ oz (300 g) mozzarella cheese
salt
pepper
sugar

1 Preheat the oven to 400 °F (200 °C). Cook potatoes in a large pot of salted water over medium heat for approx. 10 min. In the meantime, cut broccoli into florets. Add to the pot with the potatoes. Keep cooking for approx. 4 min., then drain. Once cool enough to touch, slice potatoes.

2 Thinly slice chili and garlic and add to a bowl. Add capers, white wine vinegar, olive oil, and lemon juice. Season with salt, pepper, and sugar, and stir to combine. Cube salmon and add to a large bowl, then add caper dressing. Toss to coat.

3 Add sliced potatoes and broccoli to the bowl with the salmon and stir to combine. Transfer the mixture to a baking dish.

4 Tear mozzarella cheese into pieces, sprinkle them over everything, then bake the casserole for approx. 12 min.

EXTRA TIP
To get even more flavor, sauté the broccoli and potatoes before adding them to the baking dish.

Savory Dutch baby with smoked salmon and horseradish

35

minutes

Fall

"This hearty Dutch baby with crème fraîche and fresh herbs is an ideal dish for breakfast or dinner. Fresh horseradish adds a wonderful sharpness to the batter itself and smoked salmon enhances and refines the dish, making it satisfying enough for a weeknight meal."

– Johanna

4 servings

FOR THE DUTCH BABY
8½ oz (240 g) flour
1 cup (240 ml) milk
4 eggs
⅓ oz (10 g) fresh horseradish
5¼ oz (150 g) butter
salt

FOR SERVING
3½ oz (100 g) crème fraîche
½ lemon
2 scallions
¼ oz (5 g) chives
¼ oz (5 g) dill
¼ oz (5 g) chervil
7 oz (200 g) smoked salmon
⅓ oz (10 g) fresh horseradish
salt, pepper

1   Preheat the oven to 425 °F (220 °C). Add flour, milk, eggs, a pinch of salt, and freshly grated horseradish to a mixing bowl. Whisk together to form a smooth batter.

2   Add butter to a cast-iron pan and transfer it to the preheated oven to melt. Carefully remove the hot pan from the oven once the butter is melted and pour the batter in. Transfer the pan back to the oven and bake for approx. 20 min., or until the Dutch baby has risen, the edges are golden-brown, and the center is completely set and cooked through.

3   In the meantime, add crème fraîche to a bowl. Mix in lemon zest and juice, and season with salt and pepper. Thinly slice scallions and chop chives, dill, and chervil. Drizzle most of the crème fraîche mixture over the finished Dutch baby. Arrange smoked salmon in the center and sprinkle with herbs. Garnish with grated horseradish before serving.

EXTRA TIP
If you can't find fresh horseradish because it's not in season or isn't available, you can stir a bit of spicy brown mustard or jarred horseradish into the batter instead.

60
minutes

Vegetarian

★

Crowd-
pleaser

Loaded roasted potatoes

"This all-in-one dish takes roasted potatoes from a simple side act to a crowd-pleasing starring role with a creamy Greek yogurt base and zesty cilantro pesto crown. Smashing the cooked potatoes allows all the craggy outer bits to get extra crispy – a delicious contrast to their creamy interior."

– Ruby

4 servings

FOR THE POTATOES
2¼ lb (1 kg) new potatoes
3 tbsp olive oil
7 oz (200 g) Greek yogurt
salt
chili flakes for serving
mint for serving
cilantro for serving

**FOR THE QUICK-PICKLED
ONIONS**
1 red onion
1 lime
1 tsp sugar

FOR THE CILANTRO PESTO
1 oz (30 g) cilantro
⅓ oz (10 g) mint
¼ cup (60 ml) olive oil
1 lime
2 tbsp honey
salt

1 Preheat the oven to 400 °F (200 °C). Add potatoes to a pot of cold, salted water and bring to a simmer over medium-high heat. Cook until you can easily slide a fork into them, approx. 10 – 15 min. Drain well.

2 Transfer potatoes to a baking sheet. Lay another baking sheet on top and press down to smash the potatoes. Drizzle with olive oil and season with salt. Roast for approx. 30 min., or until very crispy, flipping them halfway through.

3 In the meantime, for the quick-pickled onions, slice a red onion and add to a bowl with the juice of one lime and sugar. Pour boiling water on top, until the onions are covered, and set aside. For the cilantro pesto, add cilantro, mint, olive oil, zest of half a lime, juice of the whole lime, honey, and a large pinch of salt to a food processor. Blend until you have a runny pesto, adding extra olive oil if necessary.

4 Remove potatoes from the oven. Let cool for approx. 5 min. Drain pickled onions. Spread Greek yogurt onto a serving plate and sprinkle with salt. Top with potatoes, pesto, and chili flakes, and garnish with pickled red onions and extra mint and cilantro.

EXTRA TIP
Don't use floury potatoes for this recipe, as their interior texture will not have the creaminess that's integral here.

Creamy potato and ground beef gratin

"You can prepare this gratin up to two days in advance and just bake it directly from the fridge. For a vegetarian version, replace the ground beef with a plant-based 'ground meat' or our lentil Bolognese on page 172."

– Johanna

60
minutes

Crowd-
pleaser

Family-
friendly

6–8 servings

FOR THE GROUND BEEF
1 onion
1 clove garlic
1 sprig rosemary
14 oz (400 g) ground
  beef
2 tbsp tomato paste
salt
pepper
olive oil for frying
butter for greasing

FOR THE POTATOES
2¼ oz (1 kg) potatoes
1 cup (240 ml) heavy
  cream
⅔ cup (150 ml) milk
½ tsp ground nutmeg
salt

1 Preheat the oven to 400 °F (200 °C). Peel and mince onion and garlic. Pluck rosemary leaves from sprigs and finely chop. Peel and thinly slice potatoes. Add potato slices to a saucepan with heavy cream, milk, ground nutmeg, and a pinch of salt. Simmer over medium-low heat until the mixture thickens, approx. 10 min.

2 In the meantime, heat olive oil in a frying pan over medium heat and fry ground beef until mostly cooked through and browned, approx. 5 min. Add onion and garlic and continue to sauté for approx. 5 min. more. Stir in tomato paste and season to taste with salt and pepper.

3 Grease a baking dish with butter. Add half the potato mixture, then all the ground beef, and top with remaining potatoes. Bake for approx. 30 min., or until golden-brown. Remove from the oven, sprinkle with chopped rosemary, and let rest for approx. 5 min. before slicing and serving.

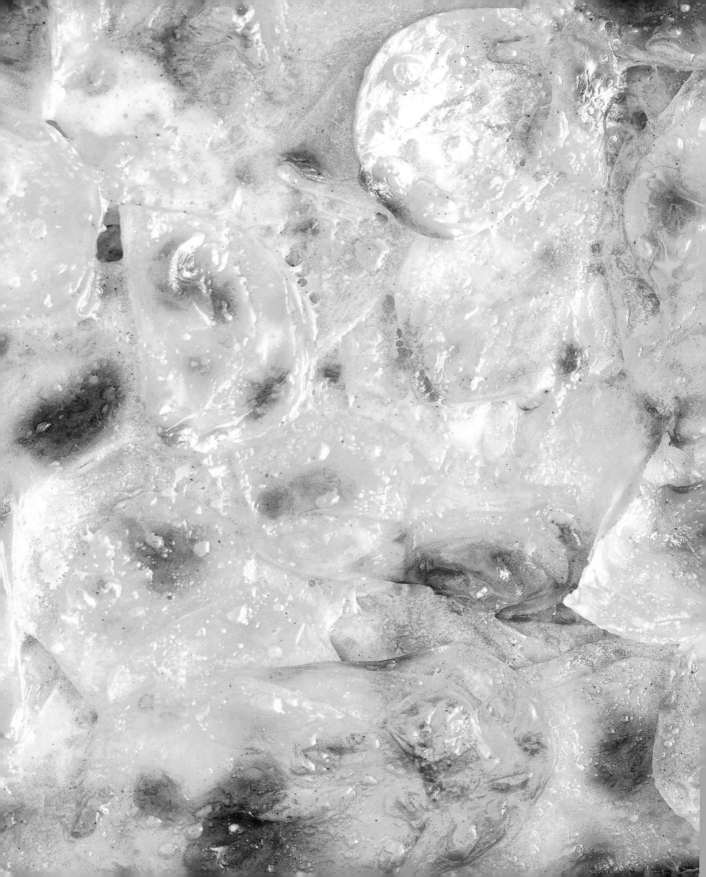

60
minutes

Crowd-
pleaser

Family-
friendly

Tex-Mex chicken and rice casserole

"Infused with flavors inspired by Tex-Mex cuisine, this one-pot recipe strikes an elusive balance between comfort food and novelty, ensuring its spot at the top of your family's go-to dinner list. It makes a big batch, but the leftovers store well and, arguably, it even tastes better the next day."

– Julie

6 servings

FOR THE CASSEROLE

14 oz (400 g) chicken
   breasts, boneless and
   skinless
4 scallions
3 cloves garlic
1 red bell pepper
1 green bell pepper
2 tbsp vegetable oil, divided
9¾ oz (275 g) canned corn,
   drained
2 cups (500 ml) chicken
   stock
9 oz (260 g) basmati rice
5¼ oz (150 g) shredded
   cheddar cheese
salt, pepper
cilantro for serving

FOR THE TOMATO SAUCE

4 tbsp olive oil
3 tbsp flour
1 tbsp chili powder
1 tsp ground cumin
1 tsp garlic powder
½ tsp cinnamon
2 tbsp tomato paste
2 cups (500 ml) vegetable
   broth
1 tbsp apple cider vinegar
salt, pepper

EXTRA TIP

For a vegetarian option, you could
swap out the chicken breast with
sweet potato or chickpeas and
replace the chicken stock with
vegetable broth.

1 Chop chicken breasts into large pieces. Thinly slice scallions.
   Peel and mince garlic. Core and slice bell peppers into strips.

2 For the tomato sauce, heat olive oil in a pot over medium
   heat. Stir in flour, chili powder, ground cumin, garlic powder,
   and cinnamon, and cook for approx. 1 min. Stir in tomato
   paste and let cook for approx. 2 min. Add vegetable broth,
   stir to combine, and let simmer for approx. 5–7 min., or until
   thickened. Season with apple cider vinegar, salt, and pepper.

3 Heat half the vegetable oil in a large skillet over high heat.
   Add chicken and sauté for approx. 5–7 min., or until browned.
   Transfer to a plate and set aside.

4 Heat remaining vegetable oil in the same skillet. Add scallions
   and garlic, and sauté for approx. 1–2 min. Add bell pepper and
   keep frying for approx. 5 min. Deglaze with chicken stock, then
   add canned corn and spicy tomato sauce. Stir to combine and
   season with salt and pepper.

5 Add basmati rice, cover, and cook on medium-low heat for
   approx. 30 min., or until rice is al dente and most of the liquid
   is absorbed.

6 Preheat the oven to 350 °F (180 °C). Add chicken back to the
   skillet and combine with the rice. Spread grated cheddar
   cheese on top, transfer skillet to the oven, and broil for
   approx. 5–10 min., or until cheese begins to melt. Serve
   garnished with chopped cilantro.

45

minutes

Fall

Crowd-
pleaser

Cheesy pumpkin pasta bake

*"This pasta bake can be easily modified to suit your tastes or use what
you have on hand. For instance, you could use kale or another green
vegetable in lieu of the pumpkin – just fry it in some oil with garlic and
a sliced Thai chili before blending (or not!) and tossing with the pasta."*

– Lisa

6 servings

**FOR THE PASTA AND
PUMPKIN PURÉE**
2¼ lb (1 kg) Hokkaido
    pumpkin
3 tbsp olive oil
1 onion
2 cloves garlic
1¾ oz (50 g) butter
3 sprigs thyme
¼ cup (60 ml) heavy cream
1 lb (500 g) rigatoni
10½ oz (300 g) mozzarella
    cheese
salt
pepper

FOR THE CHEESE MIXTURE
3½ oz (100 g) Parmesan
    cheese
1 lb (500 g) ricotta
1 cup (240 ml) heavy cream
salt
pepper

EXTRA TIP
You can use any
medium-size pasta for
this recipe, like rigatoni,
penne, or orecchiette.
For a vegetarian version,
skip the Parmesan
cheese.

1 Preheat the oven to 400 °F (200 °C). Core and dice Hokkaido
   pumpkin and add to a baking sheet. Drizzle with olive oil and
   season with salt and pepper. Bake for approx. 20–25 min., or until
   soft. Remove from the oven, and increase the temperature to
   450 °F (230 °C).

2 Peel and mince onion and garlic. Melt butter in a frying pan over
   medium heat and fry onion for approx. 2 min., or until translucent.
   Add garlic and fry for approx. 1–2 min., then remove from heat.
   Add baked pumpkin, onion, garlic, thyme, and heavy cream to
   a large bowl. Use an immersion blender to blend until creamy.
   Season with salt and pepper to taste.

3 Bring a pot of salted water to a boil. Cook pasta according to
   the package instructions until al dente. Before draining, reserve
   approx. ⅔ cup (150 ml) of the pasta cooking water and set aside.

4 While the pasta cooks, grate Parmesan cheese into a bowl with
   ricotta cheese and heavy cream. Season generously with salt and
   pepper to taste.

5 Add cooked pasta and one-third of the pumpkin mixture to a large
   bowl and stir to combine. Add as much of the pasta water as
   needed to create a creamy sauce that entirely coats the pasta.

6 Cover the bottom of a baking dish with a few spoonfuls of the
   pumpkin purée. Add half the pasta mixture on top, then cover
   it with half the remaining pumpkin mixture. Add half the cheese
   mixture and tear half the mozzarella cheese over the top. Repeat
   this step with the remaining ingredients, ending with the remaining
   pieces of mozzarella cheese. Season with salt and pepper, then
   bake for approx. 10–15 min., or until the mozzarella is golden-
   brown.

1

2

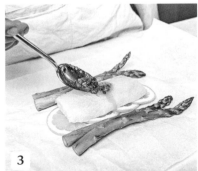

3

Parchment-baked fish with artichokes

Spring

"Wrapping ingredients in parchment before baking ensures that none of the flavors or liquids escape and creates a super aromatic, moist environment for everything to steam together."

– Christian

2 servings

10 stalks green
  asparagus
1 lemon
5 jarred artichoke
  hearts
2 sprigs parsley
1 clove garlic
2 tbsp olive oil
1 tbsp capers
2 halibut filets
salt
pepper
baguette for serving

1 Preheat the oven to 400 °F (200 °C). Trim off the woody ends of the asparagus and halve the spears widthwise. Thinly slice lemon. Drain artichoke hearts and cut into quarters. Mince parsley.

2 Peel garlic and add to a mortar and pestle. Season generously with salt and pepper. Crush until a thick paste forms. Add olive oil and capers. Stir together to combine, crushing very lightly to break up the capers a little bit.

3 Lay half the lemon slices on a piece of parchment paper with half the asparagus, one halibut fillet, half the garlic-caper mixture, and half the artichoke hearts. Fold into a parcel by bringing the long edges up, folding together towards you, and then tucking and folding the sides underneath the parcel (secure with cooking string if needed). Repeat with the remaining ingredients on another piece of parchment paper. Carefully transfer parchment parcels to a baking sheet and bake for approx. 10–12 min. Delicately open the parchment parcels and top with parsley before serving.

EXTRA TIP
If asparagus isn't in season, use pumpkin or squash, tomatoes, zucchini, or scallions instead.

60 minutes

Crowd-pleaser

From the community

Cheesy zucchini and bell pepper pasta bake

"This recipe from our community member Mary-Linh is a simple but extremely versatile dish. It can be easily modified to your taste or whichever vegetables are currently in season and whichever pasta shape you have on hand."

– Devan

4 servings

1 zucchini
1 red onion
1 yellow bell pepper
2 cloves garlic
4½ oz (125 g) mozzarella cheese
1 tbsp olive oil
2 tsp dried oregano
14 oz (400 g) canned whole tomatoes
8 oz (225 g) farfalle
2 oz (50 g) Parmesan cheese
salt
pepper
basil for serving

1 Cut zucchini lengthwise, and then slice into half-moons. Peel and slice red onion. Chop bell pepper, peel and mince garlic, and slice mozzarella.

2 Add olive oil to a frying pan over medium heat and sauté onion until translucent. Add dried oregano and garlic and sauté for approx. 2 min. Add canned crushed tomatoes, season generously with salt and pepper, and let simmer for approx. 10 min.

3 Preheat the oven to 350 °F (180 °C). Cook pasta in a pot of boiling salted water according to package instructions until al dente, then drain and mix with tomato sauce, zucchini, and bell pepper. Transfer the pasta mixture to a baking dish. Top with mozzarella and grated Parmesan cheese. Bake for approx. 25 min., then let cool for 10 min. Serve garnished with basil.

EXTRA TIP
Scan this QR code to read everything on the most common casserole mistakes and how to avoid them.

50

minutes

Crowd-
pleaser

Family-
friendly

Ricotta and spinach cannelloni

"Preparing Italian cannelloni is easier than you might think. To save time and energy, use fresh lasagna sheets, as they don't need to be precooked before being filled and rolled. If you use dry cannelloni pasta, you'll need to account for a longer baking time, approx. 45 min. You'll also need to prepare the sauce with a bit more liquid so the pasta can cook properly. I'd recommend a simple green salad, a glass of red wine, and good company to complete this meal!"

– Johanna

4 servings

FOR THE CANNELLONI
1 onion
1 clove garlic
14 oz (400 g) spinach
10½ oz (300 g) ricotta
6 fresh lasagna sheets
1½ oz (40 g) Parmesan
  cheese
4½ oz (125 g) mozzarella
  cheese
salt
pepper
nutmeg
vegetable oil for frying

FOR THE TOMATO SAUCE
1 lemon
7 oz (200 g) tomato purée
1 tbsp tomato paste
salt
pepper
sugar

FOR THE BÉCHAMEL SAUCE
3 tbsp butter
2 tbsp flour
1¼ cup (300 ml) milk
salt
pepper
nutmeg

EXTRA TIP
For a vegetarian version,
leave out the Parmesan
cheese.

1 Preheat the oven to 400 °F (200 °C). Peel and mince onion and garlic. Chop spinach. Heat vegetable oil in a frying pan over medium heat. Add half the onion and garlic and fry for approx. 2 min., or until translucent. Add spinach and sautè until just wilted, approx. 2 min. Remove from heat and drain in a sieve.

2 For the tomato sauce, juice the lemon. Heat some vegetable oil in another frying pan and fry the remaining onion and garlic. Add tomato purée, tomato paste, and lemon juice, and season with salt, pepper, and sugar to taste. Stir and let simmer over medium-low heat until reduced.

3 For the béchamel sauce, melt butter in a saucepan. Whisk in flour and milk and stir until creamy. Season with salt, pepper, and freshly grated nutmeg to taste.

4 Transfer drained spinach to a bowl and add ricotta. Mix well and season with salt, pepper, and freshly grated nutmeg to taste.

5 Grease the bottom of a baking dish and add tomato sauce and half the béchamel sauce. Add some of the spinach-ricotta mixture to the lower third of a fresh lasagna sheet and carefully roll it together. Transfer the roll to the baking dish, seam-side down. Repeat the process with the remaining lasagna sheets and spinach filling.

6 Cover the rolls with the rest of the béchamel sauce. Sprinkle with freshly grated Parmesan cheese. Tear the mozzarella into small pieces and place on top. Bake for approx. 20 min., or until the pasta is cooked through and the cheese is golden brown. Allow to cool for a few minutes before serving.

45
minutes

Vegan

Make
ahead

Ratatouille

*"When I'm making a simple recipe, I always aim to do one thing,
and one thing only: Use the best, freshest produce. Do so here
and there'll be nothing stopping you from enjoying this vibrant,
summer-vacation-feeling, classic dish."*

– Lisa

4 servings

1 yellow bell pepper
1 onion
2 cloves garlic
5 sprigs basil
1 eggplant
1 zucchini
1 tsp salt
5 tbsp olive oil, divided
28 oz (800 g) canned whole
  tomatoes
1 tsp sugar
salt
pepper
sourdough bread for
  serving

1 Core and dice bell pepper. Peel and mince onion and thinly slice garlic. Pick basil leaves from sprigs, then mince basil stems. Chop eggplant and zucchini into bite-size chunks, then add to a bowl and season with salt.

2 Heat half the olive oil in an ovenproof pan over medium heat. Add onion and bell pepper and fry for approx. 5 min., or until just softened. Add garlic and chopped basil stems and let cook until fragrant. Add canned whole tomatoes and let simmer for a few minutes, using your cooking spoon to break them apart. Reduce heat to medium-low. Season tomato sauce with salt, pepper, and sugar and let simmer until thickened, approx. 10 min.

3 Preheat the oven to 400 °F (200 °C). Heat remaining olive oil in a frying pan over medium heat. Transfer eggplant and zucchini to a sieve to drain any liquid and pat the pieces dry with paper towels. Fry eggplant and zucchini in the frying pan until browned.

4 Add fried eggplant and zucchini to the tomato sauce and mix. Bake for approx. 15–20 min., or until vegetables are very soft. Garnish with basil leaves and serve with toasted sourdough bread.

Sweet potato, spinach, and feta frittata

40
minutes

Crowd-pleaser

Make ahead

"As long as you have eggs, milk, cheese, and some vegetables stocked in the fridge and pantry, you have everything you need to throw together a frittata. It's a light, easy meal that tastes just as good for dinner as for breakfast."

– Johanna

4 servings

10½ oz (300 g) sweet potatoes
1 onion
1 clove garlic
8 eggs
¾ cup (180 ml) milk
1¾ oz (50 g) bacon
3 tbsp vegetable oil
3½ oz (100 g) baby spinach
½ tsp ground nutmeg
3½ oz (100 g) feta cheese
½ tsp salt
½ tsp pepper
vegetable oil for greasing

1 Preheat the oven to 350 °F (180 °C). Peel and thinly slice sweet potatoes with a mandoline. Peel and mince onion and garlic. Add eggs, milk, salt, and pepper to a bowl, and whisk to combine. Chop bacon.

2 Heat vegetable oil in a large frying pan over medium heat. Add onion, bacon, and garlic and fry for approx. 2–3 min., or until onions are translucent. Add spinach and ground nutmeg, and sauté until spinach is wilted.

3 Grease a baking dish with vegetable oil, then line the bottom and sides with overlapping slices of sweet potato. Keep layering to use up all the potato slices. Add the spinach filling and pour the egg mixture over the top. Crumble feta cheese over everything and bake for approx. 25 min. Let cool for approx. 5 min. before slicing and serving.

Acknowledgments

This cookbook is a product of the Kitchen Stories community, from the creative team who brought it to life with recipes, stories, and visuals, to the users who've cooked with us throughout the years. We couldn't have done it without you.

First, a big thank you to the people on the front lines of this project:

To Julia Stephan and Devan Grimsrud, the tireless editors who executed our vision for this book day in and day out, and did so flawlessly.

To our designers, Kat Pihl, Ivette Uy, and Amina Urkumbayeva, for transforming our digital product into something we can (and will) hold on to.

To Lenja Marten for her organizational wizardry, which kept this project on track and ensured every team member had what they needed to succeed.

To Aurore Caussade and Wioleta Piotrowska, the photographers behind the sensational (and hunger-inducing) images that fill these pages.

To our chefs, Christian Ruß and Johanna Reder, for testing every recipe in this book and contributing their own fair share of ideas to its pages.

To Julie Myers, our Head of Creative, who has put her heart into this project, encouraging our team to create their very best work every step of the way.

And of course, to every editor and creative team member who enriched this book with their stories and recipes, especially Ruby Goss, Xueci Cheng, Lisa Schölzel, and Kristin Bothor. It's all the better for them.

Of course, we also couldn't have pulled any of this off without the team at Penguin, especially Elisabeth Schmitten, our editor. Thank you for collaborating with us so well and making our first cookbook experience a delight.

We'd also like to thank Lukas Großmann for his impeccable assistance with set and food styling, and all of the interns and working students who supported us in countless ways throughout this process.

And lastly, to our community of home cooks around the world: Thank you, simply, for cooking with us. There's no higher honor for us than that.

Verena & Mengting

Index

 Download the award-winning app for mobile, tablet, or TV from the App Store or Google Play, or find us on Amazon Echo – and get cooking today!

About our App

Everyday cooking inspiration

Since 2014, Kitchen Stories has encouraged cooks around the world to whip up fantastic meals at home with inspiring video-based recipes and tutorials, step-by-step photo instructions, and captivating food stories. Millions of users have since discovered their favorite foolproof recipes with us, developed and tested by our team of experienced chefs and editors.

Your trusted kitchen assistant

To make your daily cooking routine easier, our apps offer a vast range of functions and features. Turn on cooking mode to tap through step-by-step recipe instructions with ease, make use of the built-in timer or integrated shopping list function, and automatically scale up or down the servings of a dish on command with our measurement converter.

Our cooking community

Connect with our international community of home cooks by sharing photos, tips, and ideas in our easy-to-use comments section, or reach out to our team of professionals for help with any kitchen quandary. Have your own expertise to share? Upload your recipes to our platform through the easy-to-use recipe uploader for users around the world to enjoy!